Living for Jesus

WHEN THE PARTY'S OVER

Living for Jesus
WHEN THE PARTY'S OVER

GREG SPECK

MOODY PRESS
CHICAGO

Illustrations by Corbin Hillam

ISBN: 0-8024-4791-0

2 3 4 5 6 Printing/LC/Year 95 94 93 92

Printed in the United States of America

To my parents,
Armand Major Speck and
Florence Johnson Speck

Thank you for your love, patience,
and encouragement. This book is a direct
result of your investment in my life.
Dad, I look forward to seeing you
again in heaven. I want to be the kind of
father to my children that you were to me.
Mom, thank you for the example of
your childlike faith in the Lord in all things.
I love you!

Contents

1

But I Don't Feel Excited

It's been an awesome retreat. Last night the Lord spoke to your heart, and you were broken. You poured out all the sin that's been eating away at you, you got some relationships straightened out, and you even caught a vision of what God might be able to do through you. Last night you felt so good!

But now it's Sunday morning. You've only slept about an hour because of the water fight, cabin raid, shaving cream fight, potato chip and pop feast, laughing, yelling, pillow war, and the horrible snoring of your youth sponsor, who has been asleep for hours and doesn't know he is covered with water, shaving cream, potato chips, and feathers. And you've been rudely awakened by the beeping of someone's alarm watch. Everyone in the room hears it except the owner of the watch.

You throw your pillow in the direction of the watch. The effort exhausts you, so you flop back down on your bed. You decide to sleep another fifteen minutes, but your bladder tells you to get up immediately. So you roll out of bed . . . AAUGH! You forget you are on the upper bunk. Fortunately you land on your sponsor, who is just getting up.

You stagger for the bathroom door, stubbing your toe twice, and completely crushing someone's Twinkie. You finally reach the door. You grab the doorknob—locked!

Your bladder flashes you the two-minute warning. You begin to pound on the door frantically. You start to sob and make promises to no one in particular. If you can just get into the bathroom, you will

- ☐ stop stuffing zit cream into your sister's toothpaste tube
- ☐ actually study for a test
- ☐ never slam another door when you're mad
- ☐ hug your Aunt Claire at family gatherings
- ☐ stop digging your brother's dirty underwear out of the laundry basket, folding them, and putting them back in his drawer
- ☐ read ten chapters in your Bible every day

The door opens, and you lunge into the bathroom. You think the worst is over, but you make the fatal mistake of looking in the mirror. It's hard to believe that you could actually look worse than you feel. You try to remember if you've ever seen a pimple as big as the one between your eyes.

What to do? You consider going outside, digging a hole, and burying yourself. What's the bottom line? You don't feel excited. You don't feel warm and wonderful the way you did last night. You don't feel God's presence at all.

Does that mean that last night wasn't real? Has God deserted you? Will this be like all the other retreats you've been on?

Thanksgiving is once a year. We enjoy it, but we don't expect it every day. If you ate every day the way you eat at Thanksgiving, people would mistake you for the Goodyear blimp. Similarly, every once in a while God may give us a Thanksgiving of feelings. It's real, and it's exciting, but we can't expect it everyday.

You see, our faith in Jesus Christ is not based upon feelings. It is based on the facts of God's Word, and the facts are true whether you feel like it or not. Imagine moving to International Falls, Minnesota. (That is, unless you already live in International Falls. Then I suggest moving to West Palm Beach, Florida, so you can thaw out.) During the winter, there will be some mornings when the sky is overcast and the temperature is thirty degrees below zero. On those days you can't see the sun, and you certainly can't feel it, but do you doubt the sun's existence? Of course not. Even though you can't see it or feel it, you know it's there because that is a fact.

On some mornings you will not feel the Son of God. Does that mean you doubt the Son's existence in your life? No. Even when you can't feel Him you know He is there because it is a fact.

Feelings aren't a good indicator of reality. So don't depend upon them. John 8:32 says, "You will

know the truth, and the truth will set you free." It doesn't say, "You will feel the truth."

In this book we are going to explore what it takes to have a healthy, vibrant relationship with Jesus Christ, so you don't have to go through those weekend highs that turn into Monday-morning blues.

QUOTE

A man once came to a preacher and said, "I was filled with joy in the meeting yesterday. Now it has all gone—all—and I don't know what to do. It is as dark as night."

"I am so glad," was the preacher's reply.

He looked at the servant of Christ with astonishment and said, "What do you mean?"

"Yesterday God gave you joy. Today He sees you are resting on your emotion instead of Christ. He has taken it away in order to turn you to Christ. You have lost your joy, but you have Christ. Have you ever passed through a railway tunnel?"

"Yes, often."

"Because it was dark, did you become melancholy and alarmed?"

"Of course not."

"And did you, after a while, again come into the light?"

"I am out now!" he exclaimed, interrupting the servant of Christ.

"It's all right, feelings or no feelings!"

(A. E. Janzen)

2

The Holy Spirit—
Someone, Not Something

Frump: Good evening, ladies and gentlemen. Welcome to "Face the Issues." Tonight we are discussing the Holy Spirit. Is there such a thing? Are you really filled, or could it be just a bad case of heartburn? Let me introduce our expert panel of guests. Dr. Bernard Freeman III, professor of theology at the Seminary of Deeper Consciences and Hair Design. Second, we have Eunice Wainright, head of the Uncivil Liberties Union, school division. We also have Osgood Teeters, a renowned author whose latest work is titled *Ghosts, Gases, and the Holy Spirit.* Finally, David Spencer, a local youth pastor. Let's get right to the discussion. Who is the Holy Spirit? Dr. Freeman, why don't you start us off.

Freeman: Edmund, we at the Seminary of Deeper Consciences and Hair Design always say that good hair design is the first step to a deeper conscience. The easy question is, Who is the Holy Spirit? But we brilliant theologians want to tackle the much tougher question of who the Holy Spirit is not, and if you do get a dye, does it color your conscience? I can say with total as-

15

surance and confidence that the Holy Spirit is not God and that a cold rinse will clear the surface conscience but to reach the deeper conscience you need a drill.

Frump: Thank you, doctor. Ms. Wainright, would you like to comment?

Wainright: Separation of church and state.

Frump: I beg your pardon?

Wainright: You cannot discuss this in school because of separation of church and state.

Frump: This isn't a school, Ms. Wainright.

Wainright: Oh, never mind.

David: Excuse me.

Frump: Yes, David, go ahead.

David: I have to disagree with Dr. Freeman.

Freeman: In which area? The rinse or the hair dye?

David: The Holy Spirit, Dr. Freeman. The Bible says that the Holy Spirit is God. Second Corinthians 13:14 says, "May the grace of the Lord Jesus Christ, and the love of God, and the fellowship of the Holy Spirit be with you all." That shows that the Holy Spirit is part of the Godhead—God the Father, God the Son, and God the Holy Spirit.

Freeman: Obviously that's one isolated verse and can't be taken seriously.

David: Second Corinthians 3:17 says, "Now the Lord is the Spirit, and where the Spirit of the Lord is, there is freedom."

Freeman: I'm sorry, I cannot discuss this anymore because my deeper conscience has fallen

	into my feet. I turn it back to you, Edmund.
Frump:	Mr. Teeters, perhaps you can shed some light on the subject.
Teeters:	Of course. I think David has made some good observations, and I would agree that the Holy Spirit is God. But it's a ghost, an all-encompassing power or feeling. It's an all-present gas, a huge impersonal thing.
David:	Mr. Teeters, the Bible not only tells us that the Holy Spirit is God, but it also says He is some*body*, not some*thing*.
Teeters:	I think you'll have a hard time backing up that statement.
David:	Have you ever read Romans 8:27: "He who searches our hearts knows the mind of the Spirit, because the Spirit intercedes for the saints in accordance with God's will"? That shows that the Spirit has a mind. The Holy Spirit thinks.
Teeters:	I didn't think the Holy Spirit thought. I thought it didn't think, but to think that it thought is something thought-provoking, and I think; therefore, I am. I don't like this thought that I didn't think about the thoughts that I thought I thinked. I think I've lost my train of thought.
Freeman:	Mr. Frump, my deeper conscience has gone to sleep.
Frump:	Dave, continue, please!
David:	Well, we can look at 1 Corinthians 2:13: "This is what we speak, not in words taught us by human wisdom but in words taught by the Spirit, expressing spiritual

	truths in spiritual words." The Spirit uses language, and that shows He is a person, not some energy force or god blob.
Teeters:	Is it my imagination, or is it getting warm in here?
Frump:	We are out of time, thank goodness. Our guests have been Dr. Bernard Freeman III . . .
Freeman:	Mr. Frump, I think my ankles are swelling.
Frump:	Also with us, Eunice Wainright . . .
Wainright:	Has any of you ever gone to school?
Frump:	The third member of our panel was Osgood Teeters, who has a new book coming out titled *Nuclear Energy and the Ultimate Tan.*
Teeters:	I really didn't think about the thought, and I think . . .
Frump:	And last but not least our very special thanks to David Spencer.
David:	My pleasure.
Frump:	I'm Edmund G. Frump, thanking you for watching and wishing you a pleasant evening.

The Holy Spirit is not a thing. He is a friend whom you need to get to know better.

"Greg, I'm frustrated because I can't live the way I ought to live, talk the way I ought to talk, or think the way I ought to think!"

"Me either."

"What?"

People are surprised when I tell them I can't live the Christian life. It is only through the power of the Holy Spirit that we are able to live, talk, and think the way we should.

If the Holy Spirit were only a power, it would be possible for me to use it any way I wanted to. But if the Spirit is God, I must submit my life to Him. This is where the victory lies. We can come to the Holy Spirit and say, "I need You. I cannot do it on my own."

How do you show people that you are a disciple of Christ? One way is by bearing fruit. When the Holy Spirit bears fruit in your life, people will notice a difference in you and identify you with the Person of Jesus Christ.

You may say, "That's great, Greg, but what does it mean to bear fruit? Are you talking about bananas,

pear, grapes, and peaches?" Not quite. I'm talking
about the "fruit of the Spirit," which is spelled out in
Galatians 5:22: "The fruit of the Spirit is love, joy,
peace, patience, kindness, goodness, faithfulness,
gentleness and self-control."

Notice that it doesn't say "fruits"; it says "fruit."
That isn't a list of traits we pick and choose from;
they all are part of the fruit of the Spirit. Let's look at
them individually. (We'll talk about love in chapter
14.)

JOY

There is a big difference between joy and happiness. Happiness is based on things, people, events,
and situations, so it's temporary.

Joy is found in the Person of Jesus Christ. If
you're a Christian, Christ dwells within you. That
means the source of all joy is within you, so you don't
have to look for things to make you happy. Instead,
you can make your situations and events joyful. If we
have biblical joy, we can't settle for the world's coun-
terfeits.

Teenagers say to me, "If only I had this, I would
be happy. If I had just a little more money, a boyfriend or girlfriend, friends in the right crowd, then
I'd be happy." But it doesn't matter whether things
are going great—"I got an 'A' on my algebra fina-
l!"—or not so great—"I forgot my locker combina-
tion, spilled my lunch down my shirt, and gave a
speech with my zipper down." You can be joyful no
matter what because your joy comes from Jesus
Christ.

"Consider it pure joy, my brothers, whenever you
face trials of many kinds" (James 1:2). You can do
that because joy doesn't come from your circum-

stances. You can have confidence in Christ and know that He has it all under control.

Jesus Christ would say to you, "You want wealth? Then follow Me, and you will be able to lay up treasures in heaven, where neither rust nor moth will destroy. You want to succeed? Great, I want you to succeed also, but not necessarily by the world's standards. Seek to succeed in My eyes, and I will open doors and empower you. Don't settle for temporary emotional highs when you can have My joy! I will develop you to become all that My Father created you to be. Then you'll know real joy!"

Solid joy needs a solid foundation, and only God qualifies for that. "Out of the most severe trial, their overflowing joy and their extreme poverty welled up in rich generosity" (2 Corinthians 8:2). May that be true of you!

PEACE

"Peace I leave with you; my peace I give you. I do not give to you as the world gives. Do not let your hearts be troubled and do not be afraid" (John 14:27).

Like joy, God's peace has nothing to do with circumstances. His peace is a tranquillity based on a relationship with Him. It's an inward calm, knowing that we are in God Almighty's hand.

"Yes, but I just saw my date talking with another member of the opposite sex."
Peace I leave with you.
"Somebody just ran into my car while I was shopping."
My peace I give you.
"I'm missing out on all these parties and other things that non-Christians are doing."

I do not give to you as the world gives.
"My family is a living hell."
Do not let your heart be troubled.
"They say I have something seriously wrong with me."
And do not be afraid.

Do you have worries, cares, jealousy, and burdens? Give them to God, and let go of them. There is no use in both of you carrying the same burden.

"Do not be anxious about anything, but in everything, by prayer and petition, with thanksgiving, present your requests to God. And the peace of God, which transcends all understanding, will guard your hearts and your minds in Christ Jesus" (Philippians 4:6-7).

PATIENCE

We live in an instant society. We have instant potatoes, coffee, pudding, TV dinners, replays, and tans.

Try this experiment. Wait at a stoplight, and when it turns green count, "One thousand and one, one thousand and two, one thousand and three," before you go. See how many times the people behind you honk before you start driving.

We are in such a hurry that we don't have time for really important things, such as family and God. Or, we take time with God, but it's not a lot of time. I'm late for school or I'm tired, so I rush through my time with the Lord.

We're also impatient with God. We want instant answers to prayer, instant understanding of God and His will, and instant results in our service to Him.

When I was a youth pastor, I had a poster in my office that said, "Lord, grant me patience and I want it *right now!*"

We need to slow down and begin to concentrate on the important areas of life. There are three important individuals with whom I want you to become more patient:

☐ Yourself

"And we pray this in order that you may live a life worthy of the Lord and may please him in every way: bearing fruit in every good work, growing in knowledge of God" (Colossians 1:10). Does that verse describe your life? That kind of life doesn't happen overnight. It's a process. You have to be patient with yourself. When things don't go the way we want right away, we get frustrated and quit. We forget that God is in the business of foundation building, which takes time.

Check out these individuals:

Moses was eighty years old before he began his dealings with Pharaoh.

Paul had to wait seventeen years after his conversion before he did anything the New Testament lists as meaningful.

John was a senior citizen before he wrote a word of the New Testament.

Sarah was so old that when she was told she was finally going to have a child, she laughed.

Abraham didn't have a son until he was one hundred years old, even though God promised him that he would be the "father of many nations."

Jesus waited thirty years before He began His public ministry.

So be patient. God will use you, but you need to actively seek Him and faithfully follow Him. Every once in a while, look back and see how far you've come. Remembering God's faithfulness in the past will give you confidence for tomorrow. Be patient with yourself.

☐ Others

You need to be patient with others, and that includes your parents. If you're sharp enough to see failure and inconsistency in your parents (or in anybody, for that matter), you should be mature enough to forgive them.

Jesus didn't just see people the way they were —as prostitutes, tax collectors, or ignorant fishermen—He saw what they could become. Instead of just looking at people as they are now, try to imagine what they could become if God got hold of their lives. Ask Jesus for His eyes, so you can see people the way He does. Then be patient with them!

☐ God

Psalm 46:10 says, "Be still, and know that I am God." God knows what He is doing. So you can trust Him, even though you can't always understand the whys or hows. We can be assured that He is working things out for His glory and our eternal good. Be patient, relax, and remember Psalm 46:10.

KINDNESS

In our age of broken promises and shattered dreams, people have a desperate need for kindness.

"Do you show contempt for the riches of his kindness, tolerance and patience, not realizing that God's kindness leads you towards repentance?" (Romans 2:4). Kindness leads sinners to Christ. It leads to forgiveness, acceptance, and understanding.

Kindness is serving one another. It is something that only the strong can do. Weak people can't be open and vulnerable as kindness demands.

Matthew 25:34-40 says kindness is

- ☐ feeding the hungry,
- ☐ giving a drink to the thirsty,
- ☐ caring for the stranger,
- ☐ giving clothes to the needy,
- ☐ taking care of the sick,
- ☐ visiting the prisoner.

When you show kindness to other people, you show it to God Himself.

GOODNESS

Kindness is outward acts that others see. But goodness is who you are inside.

To pursue goodness is to pursue God, not man. "Am I now trying to win the approval of men, or of God? Or am I trying to please men? If I were still trying to please men, I would not be a servant of Christ" (Galatians 1:10).

We should always be more concerned with God's opinion of us than man's. When we develop goodness, it will show itself as kindness to others and a deep love for our Lord. (See how these specific attributes combine into one fruit?)

FAITHFULNESS

A faithful person is dependable. If you are faithful you can be trusted to do exactly as you promise. How can we become more faithful? Let me make three suggestions:

☐ Understand that faithfulness is from God.

It is God's nature to be faithful and our nature to be unreliable. When is the last time God let you down? He never does! Things may happen in our lives that we don't understand or even like, but God is always faithful. "The one who calls you is faithful and he will do it" (1 Thessalonians 5:24).

☐ Ask God to help you mean what you say.

When we are faithful, God can use us to impact other people's lives because others can count on us. Our word will mean something.

I speak at a lot of Christian school spiritual emphasis weeks. Many Christian schools have a life-style statement that the students have to sign, stating that they won't . . .

> dance,
> go to movies,
> smoke,
> drink,
> eat,
> sleep,
> snore,
> spit,
> or skip.

Oops, I got a little carried away, but you get the idea. Some of my friends blow the statement off, saying, "Well, I'll sign it, but then I'll do what I want." If you do that, you are not being faithful. If your word doesn't mean anything, you don't mean anything because you are your word. If we are faithful, people will be able to trust us. We can be trusted to keep secrets, take care of things, and follow through. People are looking for friends they can count on.

☐ Faithfulness is not just something you do; it is something you are.

Faithfulness is a lifestyle. It shows itself in our relationships.

God. We talk a lot about the need to trust God, but do you know that the Lord is trusting you? He is trusting you to live in a way that will bring Him honor and respect.

Others. Faithfulness needs to be lived at home by

- following through on your promises
- always telling the truth
- being dependable
- doing what needs to be done
- seeking to make your parents look good in the eyes of others by your actions and words

The closer you are to God, the better you will be able to do those acts of faithfulness. The further you are from the Lord, the more likely you'll be to ignore your parents.

What are you doing with the gifts God has given you? Discover your gifts, develop them, and allow God to use them through you. But don't compare yourself with anyone else. Often we look at others and think we're letting God down because we aren't doing the same things they are doing. But God doesn't need another Billy Graham, Josh McDowell, or Jim Allen (he is a friend, and I promised I would mention his name in this book). God wants you! You have special gifts, talents, and abilities. Accept responsibility for what God has given you.

GENTLENESS

Our world idolizes strength. Look at our advertisements and products. If you were looking for a car, you might buy a . . .

Plymouth Laser	Eagle Talon
Chrysler LeBaron and	Chevrolet Beretta
Imperial	Pontiac Firebird
Jeep Wrangler	Buick Laserjet
Corvette Stingray	Dodge Dynasty

Ford Thunderbird

Those sound pretty impressive, don't they? The names themselves give off a feeling of strength. But imagine driving a . . .

Plymouth Pussy Willow	Beaver Tail
Chrysler Cream	Chevrolet Cringer
Jeep Wimpy	Pontiac Slug
Corvette Carp	Buick Buttercup
Dodge Dork	Ford Hummingbird

When we make the claim that true strength is found in gentleness, the world laughs. The world says that strength is what you are on the outside. But God says real strength is found on the inside; it's part of your character.

How can you develop gentleness?

☐ Submit to God.

If you are looking for a man with power, look no further than Jesus Christ. He raised Lazarus from the dead, healed lepers, and made the blind to see. He stood up to the Pharisees and Sadducees and defeated Satan one-on-one in the desert. The Man was powerful!

Yet He was incredibly gentle. See the children flocking to Him, the tears in His eyes, His kindness to the adulterous woman and doubting Thomas, His suffering in solitude.

Gentleness is not weakness; it is strength under control. The only way we learn gentleness and humility is by submitting to the Holy Spirit.

☐ Be teachable.

To become gentle, we have to be listeners. James wrote, "My dear brothers, take note of this: Everyone should be quick to listen, slow to speak and slow to become angry" (1:19). Gentleness is something that can be learned, but we need to listen to God. Scripture has a lot to say about being gentle.

But we have to do more than listen. "Do not merely listen to the word, and so deceive yourselves. Do what it says" (James 1:22). We must apply the Word of God to our lives.

☐ Be a servant.

"Do nothing out of selfish ambition or vain conceit, but in humility consider others better than yourselves. Each of you should look not only to your own interests, but also to the interests of others" (Philippians 2:3-4). Gentleness shows itself in acts of love toward others.

Gentleness may not be cheered by sports magazines or Madison Avenue, but it is honored by God.

SELF-CONTROL

I would just as soon skip this area because this is where I need to grow the most.

Self-control is the ability to say yes to the things that are good, right, and pleasing to God and no to the things that are sinful, bad, and dishonoring to the Lord.

Let's look at some specific areas where we need to practice self-control.

☐ Your body
"Do you not know that your body is a temple of the Holy Spirit, who is in you, whom you have received from God? You are not your own; you were bought at a price. Therefore honor God with your body" (1 Corinthians 6:19-20).

Do you know that you can honor God by taking care of your body? This is a hard subject for me because I have a problem with my weight. "What do you mean, Greg?" you ask. I do not eat to live; I live to eat. That has a negative effect on my body.

It's important to take care of your body. For example, get enough rest, don't eat too much or too little, and get some exercise. Watch what you put into your body such as alcohol, drugs, and tobacco because they can cause tremendous damage. That takes self-control. It's not easy, I *know*, but it is possible.

Major organizations such as Planned Parenthood seem to think you are just like little rabbits. They say you have no control over your sex drive, so the best we can do is give you stuff so you won't get pregnant. Give me a break! You are somebody, not something. Everyone can have self-control in this area. I have written a book called *Sex, It's Worth Waiting For*, which deals with this area. I know it's not easy to be sexually pure, but nothing of worth or value is ever easy.

☐ The tongue
"We all stumble in many ways. If anyone is never at fault in what he says, he is a perfect man, able to keep his whole body in check" (James 3:2).

What comes out of your mouth is important. You need to get rid of

- gossip
- swearing
- blasphemy (using God's name as a swear word)
- dirty jokes
- ridicule
- lying

There is an old saying that says, "Be sure brain is turned on before putting mouth in gear." We get ourselves into trouble when we speak before we think. My parents used to say to me, "Greg, when you're angry always count to ten before you speak." I never really understood that concept. I would get mad, count to ten as fast as I could by twos, skipping numbers that began with letters *t* or *f*, and then explode. Eventually I learned the importance of having my intellect control my emotions, not the other way around. So think, think, think before you speak!

☐ Finances

"Honor the Lord with your wealth, with the firstfruits of all your crops; then your barns will be filled to overflowing, and your vats will brim over with new wine" (Proverbs 3:9-10).

I know you have a prestigious, high-paying executive job at Wendy's, and you are bringing in the big bucks. . . well, regardless of how much you're making, I would like you to divide it into four parts.

God. You should take a portion of your money right off the top and give it to God. One of the best ways to do that is to support your local church.

Others. Put away some money each month to help those less fortunate than you. Maybe buy some food, clothes, or other necessities for families or individuals in need. For example, you can "adopt" a child overseas and support him or her.

Save. Open a bank account, and save some money each month. You can save for your college education, a car, a vacation, the future, and so on.

Spend. Then set aside a certain amount each month to spend on yourself. This would be for buying stuff, going on dates, and paying bills.

☐ Time

"Be very careful, then, how you live—not as unwise but as wise, making the most of every opportunity, because the days are evil" (Ephesians 5:15-16).

We need to reestablish our priorities in this area. Have you ever asked yourself, "What do my priorities need to be right now?" As a teenager, your first three priorities ought to be:

1. *God.* You need to spend enough personal time alone with Him to develop an intimate relationship.
2. *Family.* Your home must be more than just a fast-food restaurant/motel. You need to spend quality and quantity time with your family.
3. *School.* That institution that you love so much —right now, are you studying to become the best possible tool for God to use?

If we broke down your priorities and listed them according to the amount of time you spend on each activity now, in some cases TV would be getting more time than God, family, and school combined.

You know what you ought to do, so ask the Holy Spirit to control you and then step out in faith. Don't let your feelings lead you. Look at each day as a new beginning. I don't know what tomorrow will bring, but today I'll commit my ways to Him. As I am empowered by the Holy Spirit, I'll practice self-control today (1 Corinthians 9:24-27).

Where does the power for self-control come from?

☐ Seek God.

Keep your eyes on the Lord, and be a God-pleaser. When's the last time you started a day asking, "How can I please God"?

☐ Be accountable.

Be vulnerable with one or two individuals whom you can trust. Tell them some areas you are struggling in, and let them pray for you and check on how you're doing.

☐ Memorize Scripture.

Memorize at least one verse each week, and it will start to make a difference in your life.

☐ Ask the Holy Spirit to fill your life daily.

God commands you to be filled with the Holy Spirit (Ephesians 5:18).

Ask God to forgive your sins, then ask the Holy Spirit to control your life. By faith accept that you are now filled and controlled by the Holy Spirit. You may not feel all tingly inside, but you will have the ability to make right choices and live a life pleasing to God.

QUOTES

We do not use the Holy Spirit; He uses us.
(Warren Wiersbe)

There must be an emptying before there can be a filling. Your life may be powerless because you have never given complete control to God's Spirit.
(George Sweeting)

An American said to his English friend, "Come and I'll show you the greatest unused power in the world!" He took him to the foot of Niagara Falls. "There is the greatest unused power in the world!" "Ah, no, my brother, not so!" was the reply. "The greatest unused power in the world is the Holy Spirit."
(A. J. Gordon)

3

Today's Dirty Word—*Obey*

G et off my back."
"You don't know what you're talking about."
"I'll do whatever I want to do."
"Nobody controls me."

We want to be independent. We want to do what we want to do, when we want to do it, where we want to do it, and the way we want to do it. We don't want anyone telling us what to do, and we certainly aren't going to put ourselves under anybody else's control. In short, *obedience* has become a dirty word.

But I have some shocking news. Are you ready? Obedience is the foundation of the Christian life. If you really love Jesus Christ, you need to obey Him and submit to His authority.

Scripture emphasizes the importance of being obedient. Our old nature rebels at being told what to do, and that's why it is crucial for us to surrender our lives to the Holy Spirit daily.

"Whoever has my commands and obeys them, he is the one who loves me" (John 14:21). Simply put, Jesus is saying, "First of all, understand what My commands are, then make your choice. If you love Me, obey them. If you don't love Me, go ahead and do your own thing."

Your response to those in authority over you is the same as your response to God. So when you rebel and lie to them, you are disobeying God. You can't say to God, "I love You," and then look at your parents and say, "Eat worms and die!"

What does it mean to be obedient? It means you are putting yourself under God's control. You are actively seeking to please God through the power of the Holy Spirit. You stop doing what is wrong (drugs, drunkenness, lying, rebellion, immorality, cheating, and beating the tar out of your little brother), and start doing what's right (respect your parents, love others, be trustworthy, give to those in need, beat the tar out of your little brother—oops, just kidding). "Be careful to do what the Lord your God has commanded you; do not turn aside to the right or the left" (Deuteronomy 5:32).

Whom do you have to obey? "Obey your leaders and submit to their authority. They keep watch over you as men who must give an account" (Hebrews 13:17). For example,

- ☐ parents
- ☐ teachers
- ☐ boss
- ☐ police
- ☐ Greg Speck (I just threw this in to see if you're paying attention)
- ☐ laws of the land such as the speed limit (I can hear you saying, "Uh oh!")
- ☐ God

The only time you should disobey someone is if he or she directly contradicts God's Word. For example, your father walks into your room and says, "Buford (if you're a girl, Bufordian), Mr. Harrison's dog is pooping on the front lawn. I want you to take this gun and shoot Mr. Harrison."

Obviously you wouldn't go outside and say, "Mr. Harrison, catch . . . Bang."

Murder contradicts God's Word, so you would say to your dad, "Listen, Dad, I can't shoot Mr. Harrison, but there are some other alternatives. I'll talk to him, clean up the mess, or build a fence, but I can't shoot Mr. Harrison."

The fact is our parents don't ask us to do things like that very often. (Contrary to popular belief, your parents' asking you to do your homework is not contradictory to God's Word.) However, a boss's asking you to lie or cheat is wrong, and in a polite way you need to say, "You dirtbag—I mean, sir, this is not right, and I cannot do it."

Early in my Christian life I had to decide whether I was going to be obedient or not. I became a Christian when I was a senior in high school, and our school had a senior cut day at the end of the year. It was usually approved by the administration, so everything was just fine and dandy.

But in my senior year there was a conflict. The senior class wanted one date, but the administration said, "No, you have to take this other day."

"Tough," said the senior class, "we are going out on the day we want."

The administration said, "If you go, it will be an unexcused absence," and they made that announcement to the school.

There I was, this brand-new Christian. All my friends were cutting class and going to the beach. My authorities were saying, "Don't go." What should I do? What would you have done?

Being a Christian, I—went to the beach. I got a tan, did some snorkeling, speared some babes, and met some fish—wait a minute, I guess I met some babes and speared some fish. Actually I didn't go to the beach or get a tan or snorkle or spear any of the above. I went to school.

I'm not sure exactly how many other seniors showed up at school that day, but there certainly weren't many of us—some women, an intellectual, the foreign exchange student who couldn't speak English, and me.

I was feeling pretty down when I went to my first-period class. This is what happened in almost all of my classes:

Teacher: Please clear your desks, and take out a piece of paper.

Me: What? A quiz? I don't believe it.

Teacher: This is a test . . .

Me: A TEST! Oh, fine. I'm sure glad I'm this "great" Christian stuck here in class, taking a test I'm not prepared for while the rest of my friends are at the beach. It sure pays to be obedient.

Teacher: . . . and the test will be worth a hundred points.

Me: A hundred points! Mommy! (My life is passing before my eyes.)

Teacher: Put your name in the upper right-hand corner.

Me: That's probably the only thing I'll get right on the whole test.

Teacher: Now pass in your papers.

Me: Huh?

Teacher: You'll all be glad to know that you got one hundred percent, and there will be no makeup.

Me: Who wants to be on a lousy beach, getting sunburned, meeting stuck-up women, and being attacked by sharks?

I found that it *does* pay to do what's right and be obedient.

> Your attitude should be the same as that of Christ Jesus: Who, being in the very nature God, did not consider equality with God something to be grasped, but made himself nothing, taking the very nature of a servant, being made in human likeness. And being found in appearance as a man, he humbled himself and became obedient to death—even death on a cross! (Philippians 2:5-8)

Jesus Christ Himself, who is certainly more important and powerful than you or me, was obedient. It's not always easy to be obedient. It wasn't easy for Jesus—His obedience cost Him His life.

Some of you have been encouraged to accept a cheap grace. If you asked Christ into your life but then went back to your old ways, you have cheapened Christ's death on the cross. Maybe somebody told you that all you have to do is raise your hand or walk forward, and you're set for life. Then you can go back to your old life and do whatever you want. It doesn't matter as long as you have asked Christ into your life.

But guess what? It does matter! It's great that you've asked Christ into your life, but that isn't the end. It's only the beginning. You need to start living Jesus Christ. "What good is it, my brothers, if a man claims to have faith but has no deeds? Can such faith save him? . . . Faith by itself, if it is not accompanied by action, is dead. . . . You see that a person is justified by what he does and not by faith alone" (James 2:14, 17, 24).

God calls us to live holy lives. You may say, "There is no way I can be holy. That's impossible." And you would be right. In and of ourselves we will never be holy. But I have great news. No matter how unholy we have been in the past, if we commit our lives to Jesus Christ, the Holy Spirit dwells within us. Since He is holy, we have His holiness within us (Leviticus 20:8). When you keep God's decrees, the Lord will make you holy. Choose to obey the very next thing He tells you through His Word or your parents, and His holiness will begin to show itself in you.

You have to decide whom you are going to serve. Paul writes in Romans 6:16, "Don't you know that when you offer yourselves to someone to obey him as slaves, you are slaves to the one whom you obey—whether you are slaves to sin, which leads to death, or to obedience, which leads to righteousness?"

It's your choice. Maybe you have been seeking after sin. If you have, pretty soon you'll be obeying sin, which will eventually enslave you. The end result? Death.

Instead, you can choose to seek God, obey His commands, and become a slave to the Lord. The end result? Holiness and righteousness.

It's good to obey God because He tells us to, but it's even better to obey Him because of who He is!

Quotes

God always gives His best to those who leave the choice with Him.

(Jim Elliot)

The greatness of a man's power is the measure of his surrender.

(J. Wilbur Chapman)

It costs much to obtain the power of the Spirit. It costs self-surrender and humiliation, and a yielding up of our most precious things to God. But when we are really in that power, we shall find this difference, that whereas before, it was hard for us to do the easiest things, now it is easy for us to do the hard things.

(A. J. Gordon)

4

God's Will—It's No Game Show

OK, we're learning to depend on the Holy Spirit instead of our feelings and seeking to be obedient. You may be saying, "I'm ready to do all that, but which direction do I head? How do I know God's will for my life?"

Some people turn finding God's will into a game show—a "Let's Make a Deal with Your Life." There are ten doors, and behind each door is a life. One life ends in tragic death, in one you get a divorce, and in another you become an alcoholic. But behind one door—and only one door—is the "abundant life."

If God's will were hidden behind a door, we should indeed be fearful of making wrong choices. One bad decision, and our life could be completely wrecked. But God doesn't hide His will behind some door.

Do you ever do stupid things to try to determine God's will? I used to. For example, I wanted to ask this girl out on a date but was afraid to. So I began to seek God's will.

One day I was driving my car, and I prayed, "Lord, if You want me to ask her out, let the next light I come to be green."

I thought that was pretty safe because I could see the light way up ahead of me, and it was red. So I was sure that by the time I got there it would be green, and I'd have myself a date.

"Wow, it's still red. Well, I'll just slow down a little. What is that guy honking about behind me? I'm going three miles per hour.

"It still isn't changing. I'm just going to turn right on this side street and take a short-cut home, even though I'm going in the opposite direction. There, now I'll turn left again.

"Oh no, that light's red too. Well, I'll just cut through the bank's parking lot. Over these cement dividers—ouch. (Boy, I'm glad this is Dad's car and not mine.)

"Stay calm, Greg, you've almost made it. The light ahead is green—this is my chance. You can't be a coward when seeking God's will.

"So praise the Lord, and put the pedal to the metal. Oh no, it's turning yellow, go faster, faster, it's red . . . Oh Lord, Thy will be done . . . faster . . . I'm through! God has spoken, and I will be obedient in asking her out. Hey, what's that flashing light behind me?"

Let's stop doing stupid, sometimes dangerous things to try to determine God's will. In many cases He makes His will for us very plain.

STOP CONFORMING TO THE WORLD

"Do not conform any longer to the pattern of this world, but be transformed by the renewing of your mind. Then you will be able to test and approve what God's will is—his good, pleasing and perfect will" (Romans 12:2).

You can't very well expect to discern God's will while you're out in left field, playing with the world. In other words, you need to be obedient. (Notice how these chapters are fitting together? Pretty impressive, huh?) If we aren't being obedient to God, we are living outside of His will. Stop conforming to the world. Stop doing what's wrong, and start doing what's right by the power of the Holy Spirit.

SEEK GOD

"Seek first his kingdom and his righteousness, and all these things will be given to you as well" (Matthew 6:33).

We need to be willing to accept His plans for our lives before we know what they are. Often we play games with the Almighty. In our minds, we decide we'll obey His will, as long as it coincides with what we want. But what we want is not necessarily what is best for us. We need to trust God and accept His will (Proverbs 3:5-6). God isn't trying to hide His will or play games; He loves us!

We ought to ask God what He wants us to do. There are two ways we can do that: (1) by studying the Word of God, and (2) through prayer.

God never contradicts His Word, so you don't have to ask Him about anything already spelled out in Scripture. On some things you already know His will.

How should I respond to my parents when they ask me to do something?

"Children, obey your parents in the Lord, for this is right" (Ephesians 6:1).

Should I be involved sexually with my date?

"It is God's will that you should be sanctified [holy]: that you should avoid sexual immorality" (1 Thessalonians 4:3).

How should I respond to problems?

"Be joyful always; pray continually; give thanks in all circumstances, for this is God's will for you in Christ Jesus" (1 Thessalonians 5:16-18).

How should I act toward those who are mean to me?

"I tell you who hear me: Love your enemies, do good to those who hate you, bless those who curse you, pray for those who mistreat you" (Luke 6:27-28).

I know my date isn't a Christian, but I really, really love him (her). Should we get married?

"Do not be yoked together with unbelievers. For what do righteousness and wickedness have in common? Or what fellowship can light have with darkness? What harmony is there between Christ and Belial? What does a believer have in common with an unbeliever?" (2 Corinthians 6:14-15).

You don't have to pray about God's will in those areas because it's already spelled out in Scripture.

GET GODLY COUNSEL

"For lack of guidance a nation falls, but many advisers make victory sure" (Proverbs 11:14).

Go to godly men and women whom you respect, and ask them what they think about the issue you are dealing with. God speaks through others, especially those who are humbly walking with Him.

If you are getting the same advice from several sources, you should be very sure you are listening to God before you do something different. For example, you start going out with someone who's a Christian, but your friends and parents tell you it's a bad relationship. You'd better back off even if you really like your date and nothing bad has happened yet.

Your parents are great people from whom to seek advice and counsel. Believe it or not—and this is going to shock you, so you'd better sit down—your parents know more than you do! I can hear the gasps and screams. But it's true.

I know you may think you have arrived at seventeen. The fact is, you are not as mature at seventeen as you will be at twenty, and you will not be as wise at twenty as you will be at twenty-seven. Maturity and wisdom come with time.

You say, "But my parents aren't facing the same problems I am."

True, but they face temptations and problems. And the ways they deal with temptations are similar to how you need to confront your own problems.

Your parents have *a lot* of wisdom, so seek them out for counsel.

BE STILL

"Be still before the Lord and wait patiently for him" (Psalm 37:7).

After you stop conforming to the world, start seeking after God, and seek godly counsel, you need to wait upon the Lord, saying, "Lord, my life is in Your hands. Please show me what You want me to do, and I will be obedient." Listen for God's voice.

Then wait for God. There is no need to worry or be anxious because the King of kings and Lord of lords has the situation under control. We spend all kinds of time trying to work out the situation instead of just waiting upon the Lord. "Wait for the Lord; be strong and take heart and wait for the Lord" (Psalm 27:14; see Psalm 130:5; Isaiah 30:18).

WHAT IS THE DESIRE OF YOUR HEART?

Psalm 37:4 says, "Delight yourself in the Lord and he will give you the desires of your heart."

What if you get to the point where you *have* to make a decision, and you still have no clear answer from the Lord?

Go to God and say, "Lord, I have delighted myself in You. I have sought You, sought godly counsel, and waited upon You. Now I must make a decision; lead my heart."

Then ask yourself, "What is the desire of my heart? What do I really want to do?"

TAKE A STEP OF FAITH

"I will instruct you and teach you in the way you should go: I will counsel you and watch over you" (Psalm 32:8).

Finally you make a decision and say, "Lord, this is my decision. If You are not honored or pleased by it, shut the doors." Then step out in faith.

Why doesn't God just reveal to us what He wants us to do? There are several reasons:

☐ God wants us to be dependent upon Him. He wants us to learn that He is sufficient for our every need.
☐ He is teaching us what it means to walk by faith.
☐ Usually we need to learn patience.
☐ Sometimes He wants to use the people from whom we are seeking counsel.
☐ He waits for the perfect time to reveal His will.

"Your word is a lamp to my feet and a light for my path" (Psalm 119:105). God directs us through His Word, but it is a lamp, not a spotlight. We want to be able to see five, fifteen, even forty years down the road. We want to know:

☐ Where am I going to school?
☐ What will I choose as my major?
☐ Where will I work?
☐ How much money will I make?
☐ Whom will I marry?
☐ Will we have a dog?
☐ Will my pimples ever go away?

But if we knew all those answers we would not need to trust God at all.

Have you ever been camping on a moonless night in a forest, where it is pitch black outside—so black that you can't even see your hand in front of your face? (No? Well, use your imagination.)

You find your Coleman lantern and turn it on. What happens? It lights up the general area around you and gives you enough light to take one step. After that step, it lights up your next step. So off you go, down the path, one step at a time. That is how God reveals His will to us—one step at a time.

Let's say you have to make a decision about college. You have been accepted at two prestigious colleges: Bethel College and Elmer Fudd University. How would you choose a school using those six steps?

1. Make sure that you and the Lord are best friends. Confess whatever sins you need to, ask the Holy Spirit to fill you, and live for Jesus Christ.

2. Begin to seek the Lord about which college to pick. In addition to praying, it is a good idea to fast. Instead of eating physically for a meal, dine spiritually. Pray, pray, pray, and pray some more. Also, read God's Word; there may be some verses that relate to your decision.

3. Talk to people you respect about where they think you should go. Spend time with your parents talking about the decision, and get their insight.

4. Be still before God, and ask Him to direct you.

5. If you don't have a clear answer from God and you need to make a decision right away, ask yourself, "What do I really want to do?" You can weigh the pros and cons.

Bethel College	Elmer Fudd University
What courses are offered to incoming freshmen?	
Chemistry	Tattooing 101
Literary Analysis	Lunch As an Art Form
Introduction to Music	Gregorian Chanting to Heavy Metal Music
Anthropology	Early Man As a Stamp Collector
Fencing & Golf	Mud Wrestling & Full-Contact Aerobics
Algebra	Paint by Numbers
What is the housing situation?	
Dorms, townhouses, and apartments	Half-way house
What is the meal plan?	
Good food	A reasonable facsimile thereof
What is the status of student loans and grants?	
A variety of opportunities for financial assistance	Huh?
What is the faculty like?	
Distinguished Ph.D.s, friendly, caring, and approachable	Mostly sober
What extracurricular activities are available?	
Wide variety of varsity and intramural sports, clubs, and social activities	We party

Now you need to step out in faith. You have looked at each school, so you make a decision.

A lot of individuals are nervous about that last step. "What if I make a mistake? What if I go the wrong direction? What if my life is wrecked because I chose school A when God wanted me to choose school B?"

When we get scared, we forget the simple fact that God loves us. We should have confidence that He will not let us blunder off in the wrong direction.

Do you love God? Does God love you? Does He desire the very best for you? If you answer yes to those questions, you have no reason to worry. (Several passages promise us that God will take care of us: Proverbs 4:11; Isaiah 58:11; Matthew 6:25-26.)

You may ask, "Greg, I am in high school. What is God's will for my life right now?" Here are three basics that are God's will for your life today.

1. Get an education. You can glorify Jesus Christ by learning and becoming the best possible tool for God to use.
2. Maintain a healthy relationship with your parents, and obey them.
3. Act justly, love mercy, and walk humbly with your God (Micah 6:8). If you act justly, you are fair and honest and act with integrity. It means you respect others. If you love mercy, you are kind, understanding, and forgiving. You're sensitive to others. Walking humbly with God is developing your relationship with Christ. You are willing to lay down your life, if necessary, for the cause of Christ. It's the opposite of pride.

"Show me your ways, O Lord, teach me your paths; guide me in your truth and teach me, for you are God, my Savior, and my hope is in you all day long" (Psalm 25:4-5).

QUOTES

If God gives you a watch, are you honoring Him more by asking Him what time it is or by simply consulting the watch?

(A. W. Tozer)

Has it ever struck you that the vast majority of the will of God for your life has already been revealed in the Bible? That is a crucial thing to grasp.

(Paul Little)

Dear God. Your will, nothing more, nothing less, nothing else.

(Bobby Richardson,
former second baseman
for the New York Yankees)

5

Prayer—Meeting with Your Best Friend

Before we talk about what prayer is, let's look at what it isn't.

It isn't a Guinness record for speed trials. Read the following mealtime prayer in less than nine seconds: "Dear heavenly Father, thank You for this wonderful day and all that You have provided. We pray for this food we're about to partake of, bless the hands that provided it, bless the stomachs that receive it. In Jesus' name we pray, amen."

It's not the "Let's be funny at God's expense" prayer: "Rub a dub dub, thanks for the grub. Yea, God!"

It is not getting into a rut and praying the same thing over and over again: "Now I lay me down to sleep, I pray the Lord my soul to keep. If I should die before I wake, I pray the Lord my soul to take."

It is not the unconscious bedtime prayer: "Now I lay me down to sleep . . . I swing and hit that ball really deep. Wow, I lost my train of thought. Let's see, where was I? Oh yeah, if I should die before I wake . . . I sure hope I put away the rake."

It's not your "Lie down and get real comfortable before I go to sleep" bedtime prayer: "Dear Jesus (yawn), I just thank (yawn) You for this wonder . . . (snore) ah, I mean, this wonderful (yawn) day that You've given me, and I just pray that You're always wonder . . . (snore)." Then the first thing you do in the morning when you wake up is (snort, stretch, yawn), "Oh yeah, in Jesus' name I pray, amen."

It's definitely not the "Let's try to impress everyone" prayer: "Our most gracious, heavenly Father, I humbly cry out to You. Where are the agrapha to help us understand amillennialism? In this world we have those who are an anathema and those who believe in animism, but it's all annihilationism. We thank You for Your ubiquity, and we reject theosophy. So I declare this prayer *nihil obstat*, and, Lord, I pray this prayer mostly for the little children. Amen."

Prayer is not writing something out so we get it perfect. (An exception would be taking the prayers of Scripture and praying them back to God.)

What *is* prayer? Prayer is talking with God. It's coming into His presence and communicating with the King of kings and the Lord of lords.

My favorite verse is Exodus 33:11*a*: "The Lord would speak to Moses face to face, as a man speaks with his friend." That is the kind of relationship I want with God. If that's the kind of relationship you want, remember that those prayers I listed are *not* the way to communicate to a friend. Think of a couple of good friends you have right now. What would happen if you talked with them the way we pray?

1. What if you talked with them at one hundred miles an hour because you wanted to get through as fast as you could so you could do something else?
2. What you just used their names to be funny?
3. How would they feel if you said the same thing to them every time you saw them?

4. Do you think they would like it if your mind kept wandering to other things during your conversations?
5. What if you fell asleep while you were talking with them?
6. Would they be impressed if you tried to show them how intellectual you are?
7. What if you had to write out every conversation before you talked to them?

When we talk with God, we need four things.

WORSHIP

Psalm 145:3 says, "Great is the Lord and most worthy of praise; his greatness no one can fathom." Worship is thanking God for who He is. It's our response to the greatness and awesomeness of God. Using Scripture is a great way to worship God. Below are some qualities you can worship God for.

☐ All-powerful
"Say to God, 'How awesome are your deeds! So great is your power that your enemies cringe before you'" (Psalm 66:3).

☐ All-knowing
"Great is our Lord and mighty in power; his understanding has no limit" (Psalm 147:5).

☐ Eternal
"Before the mountains were born or you brought forth the earth and the world, from everlasting to everlasting you are God" (Psalm 90:2).

☐ Faithful
"The Lord is faithful to all his promises and loving toward all he has made" (Psalm 145:13).

☐ Good
   "Give thanks to the Lord, for he is good. His love endures forever" (Psalm 136:1).

It is good to worship God. Being on my knees is a good way to humble myself before the King of kings. If you haven't worshiped in a while, get off by yourself and spend some time doing it today.

CONFESS

"If we confess our sins, he is faithful and just and will forgive us our sins and purify us from all unrighteousness" (1 John 1:9).

If your sin only affected other people, you could get away with it as long as no one found out. But your sin is first and foremost against God (see Psalm 51:4). Confession is admitting to God that you have sinned. It is your response to God's holiness. To confess means to agree with. You come to God and agree with Him that you were wrong and tell Him that you are sorry.

You cannot hide, rationalize, or excuse your sin before God. Instead, He demands your repentance. Repenting is not "Oh, please forgive me, God, so I don't feel guilty so I can do it again next Friday night." Repentance says, "Lord, I'm so sorry, and by Your strength and power I want to be different."

When you sin, deal with it immediately. Some of you wait days, weeks, and even months. Some of you only ask God for forgiveness at winter and summer camps. DON'T WAIT! When you sin, deal with it at that moment. Agree with God that you were wrong, tell Him you're sorry, and if necessary, apologize to other individuals.

GIVE THANKS

"Enter his gates with thanksgiving and his courts with praise; give thanks to him and praise his name" (Psalm 100:4).

Thank God for all He has done for you. God does many things for us daily, yet we are quick to complain and slow to give thanks.

How would you feel if every time I talked to you I said, "I want that. Give me this! I need those, and hurry up 'cause I want it now!" You would get tired of me pretty quickly if I always did that but never thanked you. When you were a child one of the first things you were taught was to say thank you. Don't forget to say thank you to God.

We have turned God into a spare tire. How many of you thought about your spare tire today? OK, not many hands are raised.

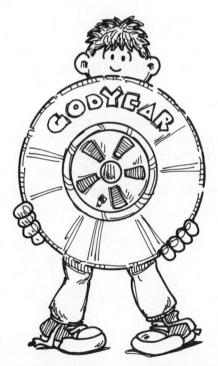

But it's 11:45 P.M., and you are speeding home (never in excess of the speed limit, of course) to make your midnight curfew. All of a sudden—Bang! A flat tire. What's the first thing that pops into your mind (other than that your parents are going to kill you)? The spare tire! Suddenly, that spare tire is very important. But only until you get it changed and you are on your way again.

That describes our relationship with God sometimes. We are kind of glad that He's there, but we don't think about Him much. When there is a major problem in our life—Bang! All of a sudden, God becomes very important, that is, until we get through the problem. Then we slam Him into the trunk without so much as a thank you, and off we go again.

"How can I repay the Lord for all his goodness to me? . . . I will sacrifice a thank offering to you and call on the name of the Lord" (Psalm 116:12, 17).

INTERCEDE (ASK)

"If you, then, though you are evil, know how to give good gifts to your children, how much more will your Father in heaven give good gifts to those who ask him!" (Matthew 7:11).

Intercession is coming to God with your requests. God delights in giving to His children. Let Uncle Greg tell you another story.

I've come to your area to speak, and there's a huge turnout because of my reputation as a speaker. The meeting ends, the auditorium clears, and all nine people go home.

Now it's time to go to the airport. We're late, but you tell me not to worry. We're going up a hill behind a slow car, and you decide to pass. Unfortunately a big semi crests the hill coming toward us. You swerve to the left, trying to reach the shoulder on the other side of the road, and you make it—but the semi crunches the passenger side!

I get to heaven, and Peter opens the door of a huge room and invites me to look around while he waits outside.

The first thing I notice is that the room is filled with presents. It looks like a gigantic Christmas. I walk over to a present and check the name tag. It says, "To Greg Speck. Love, God."

Hey, that's addressed to me! How come I never got that present? I go to the next present, and it says the same thing. Every present is the same; they are all to me from God.

I find Peter and ask him if I can talk with the Lord. He smiles and leads the way. All of a sudden, there I am before the Lord. I drop to my knees with my face to the floor. He speaks so kindly and lovingly that I am put at ease. I ask, "Why didn't I get any of those presents?"

The Lord says, "Because you didn't ask Me."

We miss out on many, many blessings because we do not ask. God should be the first Person we turn to when we have needs or problems. The Bible says, "Seek *first* the kingdom of God" (Matthew 6:33). Not fourth or even second—first.

What was in all those boxes? Was there a Corvette, an $800 suit, a large bank account, and an assortment of other adult toys? NO!

The boxes were filled with met needs, not only in my life but in the lives of others—jobs supplied, salvation for others, healing from sickness, food, clothing, and so on.

God wants to supply our needs, but we need to pray more. My friend Louie Inks, the head of Reign Ministries International, says, "Don't talk about prayer

. . . pray!" We do not have because we do not ask. (See Matthew 21:22; Mark 11:24; John 15:7; 1 John 3:21-22.)

You ask, "Greg, does God always answer prayer?"

Without hesitation I say, "Yes!"

"Ah ha! But God didn't answer my prayer."

To which I reply, "You are wrong!"

God *always* answers prayer. But He does it in one of four ways.

☐ No.

You may not like it, but no is an answer. God desires the very best for you, and He can see the whole picture. At this very moment God sees the day you were born and the day you will die and every day in between. If you ask Him something, He may say no because He can see the long-range effects of your request.

☐ Go.

This means yes. Good request; here is the answer.

☐ Slow.

Good request, bad timing. You pray that God will heal someone, but nothing happens right away. God may be saying that it's a good request and He will heal the person. However, because something needs to take place in his or her life or in the lives of others, it won't happen for a while.

☐ Grow.

It's a good request, but you're not spiritually ready. For example, if you pray, "Please, God, give me a boyfriend, please, please, please," God may say, "OK, but you need to mature spiritually first. You're not ready for that kind of relationship yet. You need to grow." My friend Frank Beach used to remind me, "Greg, God's delays are not always His denials." So be patient.

Sometimes there are roadblocks to answered prayer.

SIN

"Surely the arm of the Lord is not too short to save, nor his ear too dull to hear. But your iniquities have separated you from your God; your sins have hidden his face from you, so that he will not hear" (Isaiah 59:1-2; see Psalm 66:18). Remember to confess your sins when you go to God.

SELFISHNESS

"When you ask, you do not receive, because you ask with wrong motives, that you may spend what you get on your pleasures" (James 4:3). Our desire

should always be to glorify God through prayer. Are your prayers aimed at glorifying God or seeking pleasure for yourself? Prayer is not a magic wand.

APATHY

We lack a hunger for God. We are caught up in religion, but we have lost our personal, intimate, vital relationship with Jesus Christ.

Have you ever been working or hiking and gotten really, really thirsty? All you can think about is getting something to drink. You dream about an ice-cold glass of Pepsi? You imagine diving into a pool of ice water and gulping it all down. You become totally preoccupied with getting that drink, and you aren't satisfied until you get it.

We need to thirst after God like that. We need to be preoccupied with Him, constantly asking, Where can I go and meet with God?

You ask, "How can I get that kind of desire?" From the Lord God Himself. Ask Him for a renewed thirst to pray. "As the deer pants for streams of water, so my soul pants for you, O God. My soul thirsts for God, for the living God. When can I go and meet with God?" (Psalm 42:1-2).

PROSPERITY

"He says to himself, 'Nothing will shake me; I'll always be happy and never have trouble'" (Psalm 10:6). When things are going well we have a tendency to ignore God. We say, "Why do I need the Lord? Everything is going just fine!"

Do you enjoy spending time with your best friend when things are going poorly? Do you enjoy being with your boyfriend or girlfriend more when there are problems? Of course not. Jesus Christ ought to be your best friend, and the best time to be with Him is when things are going well.

LACK OF RESPECT

Sometimes we insult God with our prayers. We forget that we serve the King of kings and the Lord of lords. So we diminish Him by praying prayers that are merely possible and logical. But God is not limited by logic or circumstances. What seems absolutely impossible to us is easily possible to God. "Jesus looked at them and said, 'With man this is impossible, but not with God; all things are possible with God'" (Mark 10:27).

It is insulting to God when we pray, "Lord, please give us a nice day." What is a "nice" day? It isn't a great day, but it isn't a terrible day. It's somewhere in the middle. Maybe we pray that kind of prayer because that's where we are—right in the middle.

FAITHLESSNESS

"When he asks, he must believe and not doubt, because he who doubts is like a wave of the sea, blown and tossed by the wind. That man should not think he will receive anything from the Lord; he is a double-minded man, unstable in all he does" (James 1:6-8).

When we ask we must believe that God will answer. Can you ask in complete faith without doubting? I can't. I always have nagging doubts in the back of my mind: "It will never happen. Come on, these are modern times. God just doesn't work like that anymore." So I'm trapped. God says ask, but ask in faith without doubting or you won't receive. I ask, wanting to believe but still doubting. What's the answer?

In Mark 9, a father takes his son, who is demon-possessed, to Jesus to be healed. "If you can do any-thing, take pity on us and help us.' "'If you can"?' said Jesus, 'Everything is possible for him who believes.' Immediately the boy's father exclaimed, 'I do believe; help me overcome my unbelief!'" (vv. 22-24).

The key is to be honest with God. The man doubt-ed, but he was honest with Jesus. We need to say, "I do believe. I have faith that You can do this, but help me overcome these nagging little doubts in the back of my mind."

Faith is very, very important to God. "Without faith it is impossible to please God, because anyone who comes to him must believe that he exists and that he rewards those who earnestly seek him" (Hebrews 11:6).

BENEFITS OF PRAYER

Once you overcome the roadblocks, your prayer life can be dynamite. There are some tremendous benefits of prayer.

Prayer glorifies God. "I will do whatever you ask in my name, so that the Son may bring glory to the Father" (John 14:13). Our desire should always be to bring honor and glory to God. That's a good way to make sure our prayers don't become selfish.

Prayer pleases God. "The Lord detests the sacri-fice of the wicked, but the prayer of the upright pleases him" (Proverbs 15:8). We can bring pleasure to God by praying. God has done much for us. We should delight in knowing that we can do something to bring Him pleasure!

God draws us to Himself. "What other nation is so great as to have their gods near them the way the Lord our God is near us whenever we pray to him?"

(Deuteronomy 4:7). Have you ever felt separated from God? Then pray! Prayer develops an intimate relationship between you and God.

Prayer brings peace. "Do not be anxious about anything, but in everything, by prayer and petition, with thanksgiving, present your requests to God. And the peace of God, which transcends all understanding, will guard your hearts and your minds in Jesus Christ" (Philippians 4:6-7). Making requests to God with thanksgiving will bring you peace that doesn't depend upon circumstances or situations. When you pray in the midst of turmoil, pain, and problems, you can have peace.

Prayer brings healing. "And the prayer offered in faith will make the sick person well; the Lord will raise him up. If he has sinned, he will be forgiven" (James 5:15). God still heals today. He is the Great Physician, and He can heal us emotionally, spiritually, and physically.

Prayer is our answer to difficult situations. "From inside the fish Jonah prayed to the Lord his God. . . . And the Lord commanded the fish, and it vomited Jonah onto dry land" (Jonah 2:1, 10). Problems can drive you crazy, but they should drive you to your knees. When everything looks hopeless, look to God.

Prayer can change the heart of God.

In those days Hezekiah became ill and was at the point of death. The prophet Isaiah son of Amoz went to him and said, 'This is what the Lord says: Put your house in order, because you are going to die; you will not recover.' Hezekiah turned his face to the wall and prayed to the Lord, 'Remember, O Lord, how I have walked before you faithfully and with wholehearted devotion and have done what is good in your eyes.' And Hezekiah wept bitterly. Be-

fore Isaiah had left the middle court, the word of
the Lord came to him: 'Go back and tell Hezekiah,
the leader of my people, 'This is what the Lord, the
God of your father David, says: I have heard your
prayer and seen your tears; I will heal you.'" (2
Kings 20:1-5)

Some people say, "What good does prayer do? It
doesn't change anything." That passage is a specific
example of a righteous man's prayer causing God to
change His mind. God listens when you pray!

"Pray continually" (1 Thessalonians 5:17). What
does that mean? Does it mean that I am actually
praying every waking moment? No, it means that I
am walking with God moment by moment so that my
response to situations and circumstances is always to
talk it over with God. It becomes almost second nature to turn to the Lord in prayer.

Praying continually means I pray at home, at
work, on a date, at school, and while hanging out and
playing sports. When I pray I don't have to close my
eyes. If I did that when I was walking down the hall,
it would be pretty embarrassing because I'd keep
running into people. You don't have to get on your
knees. And you don't have to pray out loud—the other
people in the hall might think you're a little wacko.
Instead, you can walk down the hall with your eyes
wide open and be talking to the Lord in your mind.

I'm going to challenge you to do something that
is very, very, very hard. In fact, I don't think you can
do it for four days without missing. Why not? Because Satan hates this, and he will do everything he
can to stop you. Here is what you do: When you wake
up in the morning, the first thing you do is say, "Good
morning, Lord!" Spend some time talking with Him,

and then conclude by saying, "Lord, I want to walk together until lunch."

At lunch spend some time thanking Him for what has happened during the morning, talk to Him about what's coming up, and then say, "OK, Lord, I want us to be best friends until dinner."

At dinner do the same thing, and then tell Him that you want to be side by side until bedtime.

At bedtime talk to Him about what happened during the day. Thank Him, tell Him you are sorry, worship Him, and make some requests. Then say, "Lord, take care of me while I sleep. I want to be together with You till morning."

As I said, it will be difficult because Satan doesn't want it to happen. If you do it, Christ will become more and more a reality in your life, and you will experience the personal presence of our Lord. You may not be able to do it for even one day, but don't get discouraged. Pick up where you leave off, and keep going. Pretty soon you'll be praying continually and loving it.

It is a good idea to write down all your prayer requests, and date them. Why? Because you may pray for something on Monday and God answers it on Friday, but by then you've forgotten what you prayed for. So keep a notebook of your prayer requests. You will be excited by all the prayers God answers.

QUOTES

If you have so much business to attend to that you have no time to pray, depend upon it, that you have more business on hand than God ever intended that you have.

(D. L. Moody)

I have so much to do today that I shall spend the first three hours in prayer.

(Martin Luther)

Men may spurn our appeals, reject our message, oppose our arguments, despise our persons, but they are helpless against our prayers.

(Sidlow Baxter)

I have been driven many times to my knees by the overwhelming conviction that I had no where else to go. My own wisdom, and that of all about me seemed insufficient for the day.

(Abraham Lincoln)

6

Read Any Good Books Lately?

PLACE: Chicago O'Hare Airport

TIME: 11:45 A.M. We were supposed to leave at 9:00 A.M., but this is Chicago, so we wait.

STORY: The story you are about to hear is true; only the names, places, and details have been changed to make this more interesting.

We finally board the plane. The passengers don't recognize the Speckman because he is in disguise. Speckman takes his window seat, and a salesman sits down beside him.

Salesman: What are you reading?

Me: Oh, my Bible.

Salesman: Your Bible?

Me: (I thought I just said that) Yes.

Salesman: Do you really believe the Bible?

Me: Yes, I do.

Salesman: (Laughing) You've got to be kidding. Don't you know that belief in the Bible is both premodern and precritical? I don't know anyone with any intellectual reputation who believes the Bible to be true.

75

Me:	(Keeping my composure but wondering if breaking his nose would hurt my testimony) That's interesting.
Salesman:	You must not have done much research in this area.
Me:	As a matter of fact, I have done quite a bit of research, and I believe the Bible to be accurate and true.
Salesman:	Well, I have studied the Bible extensively. It is interesting and in places inspiring, but it is hardly true. Any fool can see that. For example, do you believe the story about Noah and the whale?
Me:	(Now I know I'm dealing with an intellectual giant.) Do you mean Noah and the ark or Jonah and the great fish?
Salesman:	I said, do you believe in the story of Jonah and the whale? Are you hard of hearing?
Me:	First of all, it doesn't say anything about Jonah being swallowed by a whale. It was a giant fish, probably a shark.
Salesman:	It does say whale!
Me:	I'm sorry, it doesn't. Here, check my Bible.
Salesman:	(He frantically looks, but he knows he's in trouble.) What kind of Bible is this?
Me:	A Holy Bible.
Salesman:	No, no, I mean what type?
Me:	Oh, you mean version. It's the NIV, *New International Version.*
Salesman:	Well, my Bible says whale.
Me:	I see, well anyway, I do believe that Jonah was swallowed by a huge fish.

Salesman: (Getting upset) That's ridiculous! It's crazy to believe a story like that. Anyone with half a brain can see it's nothing more than a children's story. Open your eyes. Use your brain!

Me: (Great. Now we have everyone's attention on the whole plane.) Just because your brain can't comprehend something doesn't change the truth that it happened.

Salesman: How old are you—twelve? Tell me this: how will you ever know if that story was true?

Me: I tell you what, when I get to heaven I'll look up Jonah and ask him.

Salesman: Well, Mr. Intellectual, what if he isn't in heaven?

Me: (Biting my lip—do I or don't I?)

Salesman: Come on, what if he isn't in heaven?

Me: (I'll hate myself in the morning.) Then you ask him!

Did that conversation really take place? Absolutely . . . NOT! I wouldn't have been that rude to a nonbeliever. By being rude I would never have drawn him to the Person of Jesus Christ. That story points to the fact that people question the Bible. "How do you know it's true? Is it reliable? Is the Bible trustworthy?"

We can answer those questions in one of three ways.

1. No. The Bible is not trustworthy. It is an old, old book that is scientifically outdated and no longer practical for our modern society.
2. Sort of. It's not totally true, but it's not totally false. Some of it is God's Word but not all of it.

3. Yes. The Bible is complete in all its parts. It is inerrant, which means the Bible in its original manuscript was without error. It is entirely true and never false.

More and more Christians are beginning to preach the second position. They say there are errors in Scripture, but they were not deliberate. Supposedly there was no way to prevent those men from making errors while they copied the manuscripts. They were just men, who got tired or careless; mistakes were bound to happen.

Wait a second! Could God have kept the Scriptures free from error? Isn't it in keeping with God's nature to give us Scripture without error rather than causing confusion by inspiring part but not all of it? That's exactly what 2 Peter 1:20-21 says: "You must understand that no prophecy of Scripture came about by the prophet's own interpretation. For prophecy

never had its origin in the will of man, but men spoke from God as they were carried along by the Holy Spirit."

If the Bible is full of errors, what person is so infallible and inerrant that he can point out to the rest of us which is truth and which is falsehood?

If you believe that the Bible is partly inspired, you are standing in quicksand. The fact is, error is error even if it's only a "mistake." If the Bible has mistakes in it, it cannot be trusted. My position is number three!

What does it really mean to say God inspired the writing of the Scriptures? "All Scripture is God-breathed" (2 Timothy 3:16). The Greek word for inspiration literally means God-breathed. That doesn't mean God dictated every word and punctuation mark or that the men who took it all down were merely robot secretaries. What it does mean is that God's Spirit so moved the minds and emotions of the writers that the words they used expressed the exact thoughts and will of God. He allowed them to be individuals and to bring their own style to the Scriptures, but it was all God's revelation.

You ask, "Greg, what evidence is there that the Bible is the inspired, inerrant Word of God?" Good question; let me give you a few evidences as to why the Bible is reliable and trustworthy.

Its Own Claims

The Bible itself claims to be the Word of God. Statements such as "God said," "thus saith the Lord," and "the Word of the Lord" occur more than twenty-four hundred times in the Old Testament alone. That means that either the Bible is what it claims to be—a work inspired by God and completely reliable and trustworthy—or the men who wrote it were crazy or liars and the whole thing is false.

THE TIME IT TOOK TO WRITE

The Bible was written over sixty generations, which is more than sixteen hundred years. It was written on three different continents: Asia, Africa, and Europe.

THE AUTHORS WHO WROTE IT

The Bible was written by thirty-five plus authors, from every walk of life.

Moses: a political leader
Peter: a fisherman
Amos: a herdsman
Joshua: a military leader
Luke: a doctor
Jeremiah: a cupbearer
Daniel: a prime minister
Solomon and David: kings
Paul: a rabbi
Matthew: a tax collector

THE LANGUAGES IT WAS WRITTEN IN

The language of the Old Testament was Hebrew. The language of the New Testament was Greek.

The writers, their occupations, and the languages they wrote in are all different, yet everything in the Bible fits perfectly together. Only God could do that.

THE TIME IT HAS LASTED

The Bible has survived through time. It was originally written on perishable material, so it had to be recopied and passed down from generation to generation. The Bible has more manuscript evidence than any ten pieces of classical literature combined. We have more than thirteen thousand manuscript copies of the New Testament.

THE PERSECUTION IT HAS SURVIVED

The Bible has endured persecution. It has withstood vicious attacks throughout the centuries. People have tried to ban, burn, and outlaw it, from the earliest times until the present.

THE PROPHECIES THAT HAVE BEEN FULFILLED

More than three hundred prophecies are made about the Messiah in the Old Testament. Consider that many of the prophecies were written seven hundred to one thousand years before Jesus' birth. And every single one is fulfilled in the New Testament in the person of Jesus Christ!

THE PROOF OF ARCHAEOLOGY

Over and over again archaeology confirms the Scriptures. One of the biggest archaeological finds was the Dead Sea Scrolls, five hundred to six hundred manuscripts, many of which contained the Old Testament. They date from 200 B.C. to A.D. 50. What is so significant about that? Before the Dead Sea Scrolls were discovered, our oldest piece of Scripture dated A.D. 826. When the Dead Sea Scrolls were compared to our copies of Scripture, they were found to be alike!

THE WORDS OF JESUS

Jesus Christ recognized the Old Testament as the inspired Word of God, and He quoted extensively from it. For example, when the Pharisees questioned Him about divorce, He answered by quoting the writer of Genesis and attributing the words to God Himself (Matthew 19:3-6). In fact, God is not the one speaking in the Genesis account. So how can we explain this?

A. Jesus made a mistake—Wrong!

B. Jesus considered the writings of Genesis to be from God—Correct!

THE CANON

The word *canon* comes from the root word *reed*. A reed was used as a measuring rod and eventually meant standard. (Hang with me because this is really deep.) Later it came to mean a list or index. So the word *canon*, when applied to Scripture, means an officially accepted list of books.

What is the canon? It's our Old and New Testament books.

"But Greg, how was it determined whether a book would be part of the canon?" It's important to realize that the church did not create the canon. The church merely recognized which books were inspired by God. Following are some guidelines that were used to determine whether a book would be in the canon.

☐ Old Testament

Is it authoritative? Did it come from the hand of God? Does the book come with a divine "thus saith the Lord"?

Is it prophetic? Was it written by a man of God?

Is it authentic? Our early church Fathers were tough about this. They said, "If in doubt, throw it out." The validity of the books that were included is enhanced because the standards were so tough.

Is it dynamic? Did it come with the life-transforming power of God?

Was it received, collected, read, and used? Was it widely accepted and approved by the people of God?

☐ New Testament

For the New Testament they used the same criteria as for the Old Testament, plus some additional guidelines. All were written by apostles between A.D. 50 and 100. The authors were Christ's original disciples, plus Paul and writers closely associated with the apostles, such as Mark, who used Peter as his chief source, and Luke, who was a close companion of Paul.

Because of those and other evidences, we know that the Bible is indeed trustworthy and reliable.

Here are some basic facts about the Bible (which I'm sure you already know).

OLD TESTAMENT	NEW TESTAMENT
39 books	27 books
17 historical books	5 historical books
5 poetic books	13 Pauline epistles
17 prophetic books	9 general epistles
929 chapters	260 chapters
33,214 verses	7,959 verses
593,393 words	181,253 words
2,738,100 letters	838,380 letters
(I counted them all)	

Now for our first and only annual "Everything I Wasn't Sure of About the Bible" test. Fill in each blank. Give yourself one point for each correct answer.

1. Longest chapter in the Bible _____
2. Shortest chapter in the Bible _____
3. Longest book in the New Testament _____
4. Shortest book in the New Testament _____
5. Shortest verse in the New Testament _____
6. Longest verse in the Old Testament _____
7. Shortest verse in the Old Testament _____
8. Longest book in the Old Testament _____
9. Shortest book in the Old Testament _____
10. Oddest verse in the Scriptures _____

Answers
1. Psalm 119
2. Psalm 117
3. Luke
4. 2 John
5. John 11:35
6. Esther 8:9
7. 1 Chronicles 1:25
8. Psalms
9. Obadiah
10. 1 Chronicles 26:18 (Look it up, and tell me what the verse means and how we can apply it to our lives.)

Score	What it says about you
10	You could teach at Moody Bible Institute.
8-9	You could star on "Jeopardy."
5-7	You will do well at Trivial Pursuit®.
2-4	You are embarrassing your mother.
1	You made a lucky guess.
0	You are barely conscious.

The Bible was written for the common people—people like you and me. It is unique. There is no book like it because it was inspired by the Lord God Almighty.

The Bible is food for your soul and spirit. You need it just as much, if not more, than food for your body. If you don't eat for two months, you are not going to feel too well. Although they can do wonders with makeup, the fact is you can only look so good when you are dead.

So how do you think you are doing spiritually if you don't study the Word for two months? I'll tell you how you are doing—YOU ARE DEAD! Right now some of you are "dead" spiritually because you have neglected God's Word. But it's not too late. Why don't you sit down to a big meal today? First Peter 2:2 says, "Like newborn babies, crave pure spiritual milk, so that by it you may grow up in your salvation."

"What can studying the Bible do for me?" you ask. There are five major benefits spelled out in Scripture. "All Scripture is God-breathed and is useful for *teaching, rebuking, correcting* and *training* in righteousness, so that the man of God may be *thoroughly equipped* for every good work" (2 Timothy 3:16-17).

TEACHING

We face many choices in life. God's Word points us in the right direction by giving us wisdom. You and I are stuck in today, and we have no idea what is going to happen tomorrow. One Person sees our yesterdays, todays, and tomorrows. He says that if we are willing to follow, He will lead us. How do we follow Him? By obeying the instructions in His Word.

REBUKING

The Word of God shows me when I've blown it. It's easy for me to take control of my own life, but all of a sudden I'm off the correct path and on a side street. The Bible shows me where I have strayed.

The problem is not our being confused about what is sin. Our problem is knowing exactly what sin is but choosing to ignore, rationalize, and excuse it. The Bible helps you to see yourself exactly as you are, without the mask you usually wear. James 1:22-24 says, "Do not merely listen to the word, and so deceive yourselves. Do what it says. Anyone who listens to the word but does not do what it says is like a man who looks at his face in a mirror and, after looking at himself, goes away and immediately forgets what he looks like."

Imagine being out on your dream date. You go to a beautiful restaurant, the ultimate in elegance—maybe a McDonalds with candlelight. There you are with your date in this incredibly romantic setting. As often happens, nature calls, and you excuse yourself to go to the restroom. Lost in dreamy, romantic thoughts, you glance at your face in the mirror.

All of a sudden, you snap back to reality. It looks as if a motorcycle has run across your face! There is a huge, greasy, dark streak across your cheek. What do you do? (Check the appropriate box.)

☐ Rub it a little, but it just smears, so you decide to leave it for now and work on it tomorrow.

☐ "AHHHH!" In a mad panic you have a total fit. You use water, soap, sandpaper—whatever it takes to remove the mark from your face. If it doesn't come off, you send your date a note: "Sorry, caught the plague." Then you climb out the window and run home with a paper bag over your head.

The second option most closely fits your response, right? No one would walk around with a greasy mark on his or her face. Actually we all have those marks, but they aren't on the outside where everyone else can see them. They are the sin inside our lives. The Bible points them out to us, and we have two possible responses.

☐ Try to clean them up, but if they won't go away, leave them for "tomorrow"—if we have time.

☐ "AHHHH! I need to deal with these *now!*"

CORRECTING

The Bible not only points out where we have gone wrong; it also shows us how to get back on the right track. "If we confess our sins, he is faithful and just and will forgive us our sins and purify us from all unrighteousness" (1 John 1:9). By heeding the correction the Bible gives us, we keep our relationship with Jesus Christ fresh and vibrant.

TRAINING

The Bible prepares us for life. We shouldn't view reading the Word as our spiritual duty, which we can forget after we "put in our time." We must apply it to our lives. Truth never goes out of style, and the Bible is truth. "All your words are true; all your righteous laws are eternal" (Psalm 119:160).

THOROUGHLY EQUIPPED

The Word of God prepares you for good works. The Holy Spirit gives you everything you need to minister to others. The world desperately needs to see Christians backing up their words with actions. As you study God's Word He will equip you to reach out to the world.

So it's important to study the Bible, but what exactly does that mean?

It doesn't mean a hit-or-miss reading of God's Word. Some people say, "I just open the Bible, read a verse, and God speaks to me." But that can be very dangerous. Let me give you an example.

Arnold Nitwit is doing his devotions. Arnold starts out with prayer. "Dear Lord, lead my finger as I flip through this Bible. OK, here we go. I'll just close my eyes, open my Bible, and point . . . here. Ah, John 14:15, 'If you love me, you will obey what I command.'

"Lord, You know that I love You. I'll certainly obey whatever You tell me to do. Wow! We're off to a great start.

"I'll just close my eyes again, flip, and point. Matthew 27:5: 'So Judas threw the money into the temple and left. Then he went away and hanged himself.' Huh? I . . . I . . . Lord, You can't mean that I should . . . uh, I couldn't . . . I'll be happy to throw some money in a temple but—hang myself? It would really wreck my day.

"Maybe I should get out of the New Testament. I'll just flip back here to the book of Psalms. The psalms are always comforting in times of stress. Psalm 89:48: 'What man can live and not see death, or save himself from the power of the grave?' Look, Lord, I understand that someday I'll die, but I wasn't really thinking it'd be today. And I'll have a hard time hanging myself because I'm afraid of heights.

"Lord, You need to speak to me because I'm kind of getting nervous. Here goes . . . Deuteronomy 12:32: 'See that you do all I command you; do not add to it or take away from it.'

"Uh oh. I'm in big trouble!"

There can be some real drawbacks to just flipping through the Scripture. Instead, you must study God's Word. How do you do that? First, it is important to understand that studying the Bible does not mean reading through it in a year. That's worthwhile for getting overview, but it isn't *studying* God's Word.

SPACE METHOD

As you read the passage ask yourself, Are there
S—sins to confess?
P—promises to claim?
A—actions to avoid?
C—commands to obey?
E—examples to follow?

Main Thought Study

Read a chapter, and break it down into sections of similar thoughts. Then make up a title for each section.
- ☐ Make the title distinctive.
- ☐ Make it original.
- ☐ Try to keep it to four or five words.
- ☐ Make it easy to memorize.
- ☐ Write it in your Bible.

God Study

As you read ask what you are learning about God.
- ☐ Who He is?
- ☐ What He is like?
- ☐ What He has done?

Action Study

Write down specifics.
- ☐ What does God want you to do?
- ☐ When does He want you to do them?
- ☐ How will you do them and for whom?

Creative Response

Respond to the passage you have just read.
- ☐ Write a poem.
- ☐ Write a letter to God.
- ☐ Make up a song with the verses you have just read.

Speak a Verse Method

Read each verse, and then say it back to God in your own words. You will quickly discover whether you don't understand a verse because you won't be able to say it back.

VERSE STUDY

Break down individual verses.
- [ ] Read the verse four times.
- [ ] What is the main thought in the previous verse?
- [ ] What is the main thought in the following verse?
- [ ] What is the main point of the verse?
- [ ] Read the verse as many times as there are words in it, and each time stress a different word.
- [ ] Write out the verse in your own words.
- [ ] How does the verse apply to your own life?

CHARACTER STUDY

Find an individual in Scripture who interests you. Look up him or her in a concordance and read all the verses about that person. There are many interesting characters in the Bible—Ruth, Lot, Andrew, Thomas, Deborah, Aaron, Joshua, Rachel, Mary, Gideon, Naomi. Ask yourself these questions:
- [ ] What can I learn from his/her life?
- [ ] Was he/she tempted?
- [ ] What problems did he/she have?
- [ ] How did he/she handle problems and temptations?
- [ ] What did God teach him/her?
- [ ] What were his/her strengths?
- [ ] What were his/her weaknesses?

TOPICAL STUDIES

Topical studies are like character studies, but you pick a topic instead of a person. Look up all the verses that pertain to your topic. Suggested topics:

☐ Wisdom
☐ Love
☐ Suffering
☐ Marriage
☐ Prayer
☐ Sex
☐ Faith
☐ Sin

BIBLE STUDY HELPS

You can use other books to help you study the Bible.

Bible dictionaries include definitions, pronunciations, correct spelling, and textual references.

Bible handbooks include overviews of the Bible, archaeological discoveries, notes on each book of the Bible, miscellaneous information, and historical data.

Concordances list topics and names in the Bible alphabetically, with verse references and practical quotes. Many Bibles have a concordance at the back.

Topical Bibles are the same as concordances except the verses are completely written out.

Commentaries include a biographical sketch of each author in the Bible, the date and historical background of each book, a summary and outline of each book's message, and a verse-by-verse interpretation. Some commentaries are for lay people, which means they are practical and easy to understand.

Devotional books are short daily readings to help you understand a passage of Scripture or topic. Some devotional books are written especially for teenagers.

I'm sure you can come up with other ways to study the Word. Avoid falling into a rut. You don't have to do the same thing over and over again—that's when reading the Bible becomes drudgery. But you'll never be able to effectively study God's Word apart from the Holy Spirit. He is the one who gives you wisdom and insight. That's why it's so important that you pray before, during, and after your study.

One quick side thought. Daily Bible study is essential, but it's OK to miss every once in a while. If you miss a meal, will you die? Of course not. If you miss one study time with God, are you going to die spiritually? No. Study the Word every chance you get, but if you miss don't roll into a guilt ball.

By now you may agree that Bible study is necessary for your spiritual health, but you say, "I don't have time, Greg. I'm a busy person, and I have all of these activities at school, then I have homework, a job, and a steady date. I just don't have time to read, let alone study, the Bible."

People tell me that a lot, but I never hear them say, "Greg, I don't have time to take a shower. I don't have time to fix my hair or look in the mirror. I'm a busy person, and I have all these activities—homework, a job, dates. I just don't have time to put on clean clothes and take care of myself physically."

The bottom line is that you have enough time to do whatever is important to you. So make your relationship with Jesus Christ a priority. Then take quality and quantity time to study God's Word.

When is the best time to spend with God? One Scripture seems to suggest that morning is the best time, but I'm not a morning person as Bonnie, my beloved wife, will testify. What is important is that you give God your best time. If it is the morning, give Him mornings. If it is the evening, give Him evenings.

I have a thirty-day challenge for you.

☐ Gather up all your secular music—your records, tapes, and CDs. Put them in a box, and give them to someone—a youth pastor, Sunday school teacher, parent, or friend—to hold for you. He or she is just going to hold them, not trash them.

☐ Decide that you are going to go off secular rock music cold turkey. Change the station on your radio in your room and in the car. Don't watch any rock videos for thirty days.

☐ Listen to Christian music. Buy some tapes, and find the Christian station on the radio.

☐ Commit yourself to studying the Bible and praying every single day for thirty days. It is important that you sincerely seek the Lord because you want to get to know Him, not because you hate this stupid challenge, or your mother is making you do it and you want to prove it doesn't work.

☐ If you do not see any change in your life, you can get your music back, and what have you lost? Nothing but thirty days well spent.

But if you see some changes in your attitudes, relationships, thoughts, actions, and spiritual condition, then tell your friend to get rid of the music, and continue to study the Word and pray daily. Write me a letter (my address is in the back of the book), and let me know what happens.

QUOTES

The Bible will keep you from sin, or sin will keep you from the Bible.

(D. L. Moody)

I suspect that the future progress of the human race will be determined by the circulation of the Bible.

(Robert A. Millikan,
Nobel Prize Winner,
first to isolate an electron
and measure its charge)

Most people are bothered by those passages of scripture which they cannot understand. But, as for me, I have always noticed that the passages in scripture which trouble me most are those which I do understand.

(Mark Twain)

The New Testament is the very best book that ever was or ever will be known in the world.

(Charles Dickens)

7

The Place You Ought to Be—Church

What comes into your mind when I say "church"?

BORING

The announcements are meaningless, the music outdated, and the message doesn't relate at all. Sunday school is about as exciting as having the flu. It wouldn't be so bad if it weren't so long. You start at 9:00 A.M. Sunday, and it seems as if you end at 3:00 P.M. Wednesday.

UNCOMFORTABLE

You don't get much sleep on Saturday nights. Then you have to sit in a hard pew wearing a shirt with a collar one-half size too small *and* a tie. Or you're in a dress, and you hate wearing dresses.

UNINTELLIGIBLE

Preachers regularly use everyone's favorite words: *epistemology, endaimonisn, fideism, heilsgeschichta, infralapsarianisn.* (Ask your youth pastor to define those words. I'm sure he'll have no problem at all.)

OUTDATED

You want to sing contemporary heavy metal hymns in church, so you complain that everything in the service is old-fashioned.

For all those reasons we make up excuses to explain why we don't go to church.

- ☐ I'm too tired.
- ☐ TV preachers are better.
- ☐ God is in nature, so I like to worship God outside while I get a tan.
- ☐ I know everything already. I don't need to go.
- ☐ I don't have any friends there.
- ☐ The people there are hypocrites. This is my personal favorite because it is so stupid. Sure, there are hypocrites at church, but there are also hypocrites at the shopping mall, restaurants, bowling alleys, and supermarkets. In fact, sometimes there are even hypocrites in public restrooms. I don't see you standing outside a restroom saying, "I'm not going because there are hypocrites in there."

What is the church?

The Greek word for church is *ecclesia,* and it means "called out." The church is not a building. It is the Body of Christ. It is believers like you and me. "The church . . . is his body, the fullness of him who fills everything in every way" (Ephesians 1:23). So the church is a body of believers who have been called out of the world and are under the authority of Jesus Christ.

Why do we have to go to church?

TO WORSHIP

"I, by your great mercy, will come into your house; in reverence will I bow down toward your holy temple" (Psalm 5:7). One of the main reasons you should go to church is to worship the Lord God Almighty. What is worship? It is ascribing worth to God. It is adoring, lifting up, praising, bowing down, magnifying, thanking, and loving God.

Worship is not like a football game. We don't show up for church to watch a bunch of "professionals" perform. Worship is participation—praying, singing, and studying as unto the Lord. We come to church to meet with God Almighty, not to watch others meet Him.

Here are two essentials for worshiping God.

☐ Hunger for God

"As the deer pants for streams of water, so my soul pants for you, O God. My soul thirsts for God, for the living God. Where can I go and meet with God?" (Psalm 42:1-2). Worship is a desire to enter into the presence of God and to hear His voice.

If you received an invitation to come to a great dinner at the White House, you would be thrilled. You would hunger for it, you'd count off the minutes before you could be there, and other people and activities would take a backseat to the event. That is how we should hunger for God.

☐ Sensitivity to sin

Psalm 51:1 says, "Have mercy on me, O God, according to your unfailing love; according to your great compassion blot out my transgressions." Worshiping God will lead us to confess our sin. Coming into God's glorious presence makes me more aware of my sin. I need to confess it immediately, so I can be clean before my Lord. Having a sensitivity to sin keeps me humble and dependent upon God.

To Pray

"I tell you that if two of you on earth agree about anything you ask for, it will be done for you by my Father in heaven. For where two or three come together in my name, there am I with them" (Matthew 18:19-20). Just think of fifty people—or one hundred, five hundred, or one thousand—all praying for the same thing! That is great power.

For Baptism and Communion

At church we can participate in two very important acts with the rest of the Body of Christ.

☐ Baptism

"We were therefore buried with him through baptism into death in order that, just as Christ was raised from the dead through the glory of the Father, we too may live a new life" (Romans 6:4). Baptism is an outward sign of your faith in Jesus Christ and your desire to follow Him. When you stand to be baptized, you represent Christ's life on this earth. As you are laid back you represent Christ's willingness to lay down His life. As you go under the water you are saying that Christ died and was buried. Finally, as you are raised out of the water you are telling everyone that Christ rose from the dead and is alive today.

Being baptized should always follow your commitment to Jesus Christ. If you have never been baptized, talk with your parents and pastor, and then take this step of obedience.

☐ Communion

"Whenever you eat this bread and drink this cup, you proclaim the Lord's death until he comes" (1

Corinthians 11:26). Communion is remembering what Christ did for you on the cross and looking forward to His coming again. The wine or juice symbolizes Christ's blood, which cleanses us of our sin. The bread represents the body of Christ, which was broken for us so that we could be made whole.

For Fellowship

"They devoted themselves to the apostles' teaching and to the fellowship, to the breaking of bread and to prayer" (Acts 2:42). Each week we have an opportunity to get away from the pressure and problems of the world and to come together with people who love us.

The Bible calls that *koinonia*, and it refers to a close-knit group of Spirit-filled believers. The word describes a group that talks together, weeps with those who weep, and rejoices with those who rejoice. They deeply love each other and make sacrifices for one another. They not only listen to each other's needs; they seek to meet those needs.

For Teaching

Another purpose of the church is to edify the members. To edify means to build up, teach, develop, and disciple. The main purpose of a church service is *not* evangelism! Some pastors today preach evangelistic messages but don't feed their congregations. They basically say the same thing week after week, and their members are dying from spiritual malnutrition. The church needs to disciple its members, so they can go out and talk about Jesus Christ with their neighbors and friends.

To Identify with Christ

"Whoever acknowledges me before men, I will also acknowledge him before my Father in heaven. But whoever disowns me before men, I will disown him before my Father in heaven" (Matthew 10:32-33). Going to church gives you the chance to identify with Christ. You are proclaiming that you are a Christ-follower. You can't love someone and be ashamed of him at the same time. Going to church is a good way to say, "Lord, I love you."

Sometimes the worst day for the family is Sunday.

You wake up tired. You try to get a little extra sleep, but eventually you get yelled at. Now you are ticked, and your parents are ticked.

Someone is hogging the bathroom, so you stand in the hall pounding on the door.

Someone yells from the other bathroom. Dad has cut himself shaving again.

Mom finishes putting on her makeup as the unmistakable aroma of burning breakfast reaches your nostrils.

You finally get into the bathroom, which now resembles a disaster area, just as your mother walks by. She tells you to be sure and clean up the mess you've made. Before you can protest, she smells the burning breakfast and rushes angrily to the kitchen.

Breakfast is a total washout, and things get worse when Dad makes a sarcastic comment that tees Mom off. You wish you were still in bed.

Mom and Dad are not speaking to each other as you head for the car. You are all in the car when Dad notices he has blood on his collar. He leaves in a rage to change shirts.

Mom wants to know if you cleaned the bathroom. You try to tell her you didn't make the mess—the Thing sitting next to you in the backseat did. Mom accuses you of talking back. Another argument begins.

By the time you finally leave for church, no one is talking to anyone. Dad is driving fast to make it on time, and Mom tells him to slow down. Dad says he could if Mom hadn't made them so late. Mom explodes.

At church everyone tumbles out of the car, each one going in a different direction. You don't see each other until the end of church.

No wonder we don't get anything out of the church services! How can we start getting more out of church?

CHANGE YOUR ATTITUDE

You can't expect to get much out of church if you have a bad attitude. "My mother's making me go to church. I hate being told what to do, so I'm not going to like it." No wonder you think church is boring. You are the church, so if you say the church is dead, that means you are dead!

Because the church is made up of people, there will always be problems and imperfections. If there were ever a perfect church, neither you nor I would qualify for membership. Ask God to forgive you for your lousy attitude toward His house and to help you change your attitude.

PREPARE YOURSELF

You can do all kinds of things to prepare yourself for worship.

☐ Get some sleep the night before. You will be amazed at how much better you feel and how much more you get out of the service.

☐ Move away from people who distract you. If you sit with friends who are always messing around, you won't get a lot out of the preaching.

☐ Sit as close to the front as possible. The farther back you are, the more distractions there will be.

☐ Pray before the service starts. Ask God to speak to you and teach you.

☐ Pray along with the prayers. Agree with the person praying, and ask God to work.

☐ Think about the words of the hymns. They may be old, but they talk about a God who is the same yesterday, today, and forever. Singing hymns is a great way to worship God.

☐ Be sure you bring a Bible so you can follow along.

☐ Take notes while the pastor is giving the message. I don't care how incredibly boring the speaker is; if he is preaching from the Word of God, you can get something out of it. Try to find one thing that you can apply to your life.

☐ If your family attends church, sit with them. You can spend time with your friends before and after the service. Sit with your family, and think about the Lord.

☐ After church, discuss the service with your family. Talking about what you heard will do two things for you. First, it will help to ingrain what you learned in your mind. Second, you will gain insights from other family members who learned things you hadn't even noticed.

REMEMBER WHY YOU ARE THERE

You are not at church primarily to see your friends. You are there to meet with God, worship Him, and grow as a believer in Jesus Christ. We need to get our eyes off the failures and center on the Person of Jesus Christ. Why don't you start helping to improve your church? You are either part of the problem or part of the solution.

QUOTES

Ask yourself, "What kind of church would ours be if everyone was like I am?"

(Anonymous)

Church attendance is as vital to a disciple as a transfusion of rich, healthy blood is to a sick man.

(D. L. Moody)

The early disciples were fishers of men, while modern disciples are often little more than aquarium keepers.

(Malcolm Muggeridge)

Someone should inform the contemporary church that the time has come to cease defining Christianity and begin demonstrating it.

(Richard Ellsworth Day)

Don't look for the perfect church. You'll never find it, and even if you did, you couldn't qualify for membership.

(Wilfred Winget)

8

This Is Good News—Evangelism

I spend a lot of time in airports, so I have seen all kinds of "witnessers." Here are my favorites.

THE AGGRESSIVE

He stalks his prey, looking for someone isolated, alone, and defenseless. Then he pounces, practically jumping into his victim's lap. Grabbing his prey by the collar, he yells, "Do you need to be saved?"

The victim responds, "Yes, I do—from YOU!"

THE SHY

This guy is fun to watch because he wants to witness, but he's scared to death. You can recognize him because he is carrying a Bible, praying, and sweating. After about six hours of getting up the nerve, he walks up to someone and says, "Excuse me."

There is no response because he is speaking in a whisper.

"Excuse me."

Still nothing. He clears his throat.

"Excuse me."

The person turns around and says, "YES?" in a very loud voice.

Now you can see panic in the shy person's face. His eyes get really big. "Ah . . . um . . . I was wondering . . ."

"What do you want?"

"Do you . . . I mean, do you . . . excuse me, do, do . . . ?"

"HURRY UP!"

"Do you know where the restroom is?" Then he scampers back to his corner, praying and sweating.

THE INTELLECTUAL

You can spot the intellectual because she reads from a Greek New Testament and carries a *Strong's Complete Concordance.* She approaches you and says, "Hello, I wonder whether you would agree or disagree that the ontological, cosmological approach to creation is only relevant to the transcendent state that Bonhoeffer and Kirkegaard asserted, although its prevalence is incongruous in Spurgeon's thought?"

Your best response is, "Huh?"

My point here is that the approach is not what is most important. No one ever said, "Go ye into all the world, and be a nerd." The best thing to do is to just be yourself . . . unless you are a nerd.

What *is* important when you share Jesus Christ? The message. You need to be able to tell your friends how to become a Christian. Below are some facts to tell your friends and some Scriptures you can use.

JOHN 3:16

"For God so loved the world that he gave his one and only Son, that whoever believes in him shall not perish but have eternal life."

First and foremost your friends need to know that God loves them unconditionally. No matter what they have done, God still loves them. The Lord doesn't just see them now; He sees what they can become if they trust Him. Beyond their problems He sees something beautiful waiting to come to the surface. As unbelievable as it sounds, the Lord of the universe wants to be their friend!

ROMANS 3:23

"For all have sinned and fall short of the glory of God."

Nobody needs to tell your friends they have sinned. As soon as you start talking about sin, they will realize that. Their sin has already caused them to give up at times. They've said, "Oh well, I've already gone this far. It doesn't matter anymore." They feel guilty, and the gap between them and God grows wider. Sometimes they try to bridge that gap on their own by being good, but it doesn't work.

Your friends might say, "I don't do terrible things. I'm really pretty good." But we all sin. Whether we sin a little or a lot, we still sin, and it still separates us from God.

Here is an example you can use. There are two cliffs with a fifty-foot gap separating them. The drop is one thousand feet straight down to certain death. If you are totally uncoordinated and fall off the edge, you fall to your death. If you're a great athlete and just set a new Olympic long-jump record of forty feet, what will happen if you try to jump across?

You see, it doesn't matter if you sin a little or a lot. Sin is sin.

ROMANS 6:23

"For the wages of sin is death."

When we die we either go to heaven or to hell. We do not die and go to Disneyland. People need to know that there is a penalty for sin: total separation from God.

ROMANS 5:8

But there is good news! "But God demonstrates his own love for us in this: While we were still sinners, Christ died for us."

Jesus Christ bridged the gap between God and man. He built a bridge across that fifty-foot gap, so we can make it across easily.

Christ, who knew no sin, took upon Himself my sins and your sins. No longer does your past determine your future. You can be different because God gives you the power to change.

JOHN 1:12

"To all who received him, to those who believed in his name, he gave the right to become children of God."

It's not good enough to believe that you are sinful and that Christ died to pay for your sin. You need to ask Christ into your heart. For example, I may take a $100 bill and hold it out in front of you and say, "I'm going to give you this money."

And you answer, "Oh boy, I really believe that you'll give it to me!"

"OK, here it is."

"Yep, there it is."

"Well, here it is."

"Yes, I see it. It's right there."

You are never going to have that money until you reach out and take it. You may believe that Jesus Christ exists, but you keep looking at Him saying, "There You are." You need to reach out, and ask Him into your life.

If your friends say, "I'm not good enough," tell them, "You're absolutely right. None of us is good enough. Salvation's a free gift that we just receive."

1 JOHN 5:11-13

"God has given us eternal life, and this life is in his Son. He who has the Son has life; he who does not have the Son of God does not have life. I write these things to you who believe in the name of the Son of God so that you may know that you have eternal life."

Not only does your friend's life begin anew, but he or she also can look forward to eternal life in heaven.

Why don't you tell your friends about Jesus?

"I don't want to offend them. Who am I to push the gospel down their throats? If they want answers, they'll come to me. They know what they're doing."

Give me a break! If your friends were dying of cancer and you had the cure, would you say, "I don't want to offend them. Who am I to push a cure down their throats? If they want answers, they'll come to me? They must like dying!" That would be stupid. You would say, "Do this, and you can live."

Actually your friends are dying a much worse death than cancer because it's a spiritual death. You have the cure, but you hide it because you think it's too offensive. You want to know what's really offensive? Hell!

You need to love your friends enough to risk your relationship with them. Say to them, "Even if you hate me, make fun of me, or think I'm a geek, I love you too much to see you go to hell, so I'm going to tell you about Jesus Christ."

Do you love Jesus Christ? You can't love someone and be ashamed of him at the same time.

Imagine being out with someone you love very much. She picks you up, and while you're in the car together, she tells you how much she loves you. But you pull up to a stop light, and she sees some of her friends on the corner.

To you:	Get down, quick. Get your head under the dash.
To her friends:	Hi. No one else in the car. Just me.
To you:	Stay down. They might see you. No, don't look up.
To her friends:	What's that hair? Oh, uh, it's my dog. (She pets the back of your head.) Yeah! It's my dog.

The light changes, she drives off, and then she says to you, "I love you so much."

You would say, "You don't love me at all." Why not? Because you can't love someone and be ashamed of that person at the same time. We'd be insulted if anyone treated us like that, but that's exactly the way we treat God sometimes.

At church, retreats, camps, and conferences we tell God how much we love Him, but when we get to school we want Him as far away from us as possible.

How do you prepare to talk about your faith?

SEEK GOD

You need to be seeking God and developing a close friendship with Jesus Christ. The first key is staying connected with Christ. Remember what we've talked about: stay in the Word.

BE FILLED WITH THE HOLY SPIRIT

We need to be empowered by the Holy Spirit. "You will receive power when the Holy Spirit comes on you; and you will be my witnesses in Jerusalem, and in all Judea and Samaria, and to the ends of the earth" (Acts 1:8).

The Holy Spirit will convict your friends of sin. He is the one who will give you wisdom and the right words to say.

USE THE SCRIPTURES

Use the Scriptures when you talk to your friends. You can take anyone through the five steps at the beginning of this chapter. But don't just give them your opinions; give them the Word. That's what will pierce the heart.

PRAY, PRAY, PRAY!

"This is the confidence we have in approaching God: that if we ask anything according to his will, he hears us. And if we know that he hears us—whatever we ask—we know that we have what we asked of him" (1 John 5:14-15).

Pray for the salvation of your friends. Ask God to break their hearts and bring them to Himself. Ask the Holy Spirit to lay upon your heart the names of three people who need to know Christ. Write down their names.

1. _____

2. _____

3. _____

Begin to faithfully pray for them daily!

Be Available

Be the kind of person God can use. When God opens the door, be willing to step through it. If you are prepared and available, God will use you. He will give you opportunities to tell your friends about Him in ways that don't seem forced or awkward.

Let's say I do all that, I talk to my friends about Christ, and they aren't interested. What do I do?

Rejoice! We are not responsible for winning anyone to Christ. We only need to be willing to speak, and the Holy Spirit does the reaping. The definition of a successful witness is taking the initiative to share Jesus Christ by the power of the Holy Spirit and leaving the results up to God.

Some facts to remember when your friends reject Christ:

☐ They aren't rejecting you, so don't take it personally.
☐ God's timing is perfect. Some of us sow seeds, others water them, and others reap the harvest. Maybe you are a sower.
☐ Continue to love them. Don't stop being their friend; instead, be patient.

☐ Keep praying. Prayer releases the power of God to work in their lives.

I wish I could take you forward in time to the great white throne judgment. There, before God Almighty, will be all the unsaved who have ever lived.

"Away from Me. I never knew you. Away to eternal damnation," He will say.

You know what bothers me about that? I'm going to see friends—people I sat next to in class, played sports with, and spent time with. I'll see neighbors, coworkers, and maybe even family members.

They'll say, "Greg, if you knew it was going to end like this, why didn't you tell me?"

What will I say? "Well, I was kind of scared, and I was afraid you would laugh at me. That's why I'm going to heaven, and you're going to hell."

Does that sound flimsy to you? It does to me. We have the greatest news in the world! Let's start telling our friends that they can be best friends with the King of kings and the Lord of lords and live forever!

QUOTES

Evangelism is just one beggar telling another beggar where to find bread.

(D. T. Niles)

Evangelism is the spontaneous overflow of a glad and free heart in Jesus Christ.

(Robert Munger)

9

Here I Am, Lord— Send My Brother!

I had just become a Christian a few months earlier. A missionary was speaking to our youth group, and there I sat.

Missionary: Depending on the season, you carry a tennis racket in the country where I live.

Me: Wow! They have tennis courts on the mission field. This is great! I love tennis.

Missionary: You especially carry the rackets at night.

Me: They even have lighted courts; this is awesome.

Missionary: Because we have these large spiders—

Me: Huh?

Missionary: —that drop out of the trees as you walk by and try to land on you.

Me: Didn't they make a horror movie about this?

Missionary: So you swat them with the racket before they land on you as you walk to the bathroom. If you smash them, they make quite a mess. It looks like a fur ball covered with tapioca pudding.

Me: Excuse me, I think I need to leave.

I didn't like spiders back then, and I don't like them today. So I decided then and there that someone else could go on the mission field. My attitude was, "Here I am Lord; please send . . . my brother!"

As I matured, I discovered that God had given me unique gifts and abilities that He could use. Disliking flying spiders didn't disqualify me from ministering for God. I could do other things.

We are great at coming up with excuses for why we should let someone else do what God has called us to do. But God has called each of us to be leaders, to set examples, to take the initiative to do what needs to be done. What will it take for you to become a leader for God? Let me suggest seven pillars of being a leader.

WALK WITH GOD

"Enoch *walked with God;* then he was no more, because God took him away" (Genesis 5:24).

"Noah was a righteous man, blameless among the people of his time, and he *walked with God*" (Genesis 6:9).

As you look at the great men and women of the faith you will notice that they had one thing in common: they walked with God.

To walk with God is to develop a friendship with Him.

Pretend I have given you an all-expense paid vacation to Hawaii for three weeks. This is your schedule.

    10:00 A.M. Get up.
    10:45 A.M. Eat BIG breakfast.
    11:30 A.M. Walk a half block to beach.
    11:40 A.M.–1:30 P.M. Lie on beach.
    1:30 P.M. Eat BIG picnic lunch.

2:00–5:00 P.M. Lie on beach.
5:00 P.M. Walk a half block to motel.
5:10 P.M. Take shower and get dressed.
7:00 P.M. Eat BIG dinner.
8:30–12:00 P.M. Watch TV and videos.
12:00 A.M. Eat BIG snack.
1:00 A.M. Go to bed.

After three weeks, I visit you. I ask you to put on a pair of shorts and tennis shoes. We go outside, and I ask you to run one hundred yards. You step up to the starting line, I shout, "Go!" and you waddle down the road for a hundred yards. Even though you are out of shape and it takes you a very, very long time, you are able to run a hundred yards.

"Very good," I say, trying to be as polite as possible. "Now get on the starting line again. This time I want you to run twenty-six miles without stopping." So you step up to the starting line, I shout, "Go," and —you pass out.

Anyone can run a sprint, but to run a marathon you have to train and practice. Anyone can serve Jesus for a week. We go to camp, get excited about serving Jesus, come home, and serve the Lord for seventeen days. That's a sprint.

But God has not called us to be sprinters; rather, we are to be marathon runners. He hasn't called us to serve Him for a week, a month, or even six months. He has called us to serve Him for a lifetime. That doesn't happen by sitting around watching TV, reading comic books, eating ice cream, and hanging around brain-dead friends.

GET INVOLVED

"From everyone who has been given much, much will be demanded; and from the one who has been entrusted with much, much more will be asked" (Luke 12:48). Jesus Christ has not called us to be spectators; we are to be participators.

Sometimes we sit back and criticize our youth programs, instead of actively supporting our leaders.

☐ First month

> Youth Pastor: Come on out, everyone, we are go-
> ing to play volleyball.
>
> Youth Group: Oh brother. Well, he's new, so we'll
> give him a break. We'll play volley-
> ball this once, but things better
> improve.

☐ Second month
> Youth Pastor: This month we are going to have a
> progressive dinner. It will include
> steak, shrimp, crab, BBQ ribs, po-
> tatoes, vegetables, drinks, and
> dessert.
>
> Youth Group: What! No ham? Well, the dessert
> had better be good.

☐ Third month
> Youth Pastor: We are going on a weekend ski trip,
> and it's going to be awesome. The
> cost for rented skis, lift tickets,
> room, meals, and transportation
> for the weekend will be only $49!
>
> Youth Group: Now we're doing some better stuff,
> but I hope he doesn't expect each of
> us to come up with $49 all by our-
> selves.

☐ Fourth month

Youth Pastor: Last month was nothing compared to what we're going to do this month. We're all going sky diving. Everyone bring a non-Christian friend, and just before we jump I'll talk about death and see if your friends want to ask Christ into their lives.

Youth Group: OK, this is pretty fun, but I'm not jumping if they don't give me a parachute.

☐ Fifth month

Youth Pastor: Before I tell you about this month's social let me report on the results from last month. We had five teens come to Christ and two go to heaven. I told you no sharing parachutes, but some were talking instead of listening. Let that be a lesson to you. Now for this month's social. ARE YOU EXCITED? (No response.) Well, you will be because this month we're going to Europe!

Youth Group: I'll go if we stay away from England. I hear it's cold, and I don't want my tan to fade.

☐ Sixth month

Youth Pastor: We had a great turnout for Europe, and I'm sorry about those of you whose tans faded. This month I thought we would all get together and play volleyball.

Youth Group: WHAT? Volleyball? I've been to Europe and skydiving. Who wants to play stupid volleyball?

You see, teenagers sit around and say, "Entertain me. Make it fun and exciting, or I won't like it." Then they complain or go to the church across town because they have activities that are more fun.

Don't be a spectator waiting to be entertained. We are called to be participators, to be involved. That's part of what it means to be a leader.

SET AN EXAMPLE

You should be seeking to set a positive example in your youth group, home, church, and work. "I urge you to imitate me" (1 Corinthians 4:16). How many of us can say to our peers, "Follow me, and do what I do because I'm following the Lord and seeking to please Him." Who are we examples for?

☐ Non-Christians

You represent Jesus Christ, and non-Christians are going to learn far more from watching you than from listening to you. They hear a lot about Jesus Christ, but they need to see you living Him. If your actions don't back up your words, your words become meaningless.

When you go camping you can build two types of fires.

• One burns clean and bright. It's warm, inviting, and people love to be around it.
• The second is the kind of fire I usually make. No matter where (cough) you stand, the smoke (cough) blows in your face. It stings (cough,

cough) your eyes, smells up your (cough) clothes, and is not very fun (cough) to be around.

Those fires represent two kinds of Christians.

- One kind burns clear and bright with a love for Jesus Christ. These are warm, caring individuals, and other people are drawn to them.
- The second kind is caught up in the world. Sometimes people catch a glimpse of Jesus in them, but usually they are so fogged up with sin and self that they are miserable to be around.

Which type are you? Our non-Christian friends are searching for answers, and we have the answer in Jesus Christ. So let's set a good example for them.

☐ Carnal Christians

Carnal Christians are our weak brothers and sisters. They claim a commitment to Jesus Christ, but they have their eyes on the world, so they aren't really watching where they are going.

I don't want to brag, but when I was in fifth grade I was an awesome kickball player. We had an all-star game at the end of the year, and I was chosen to start at center field for our team.

It was the fifth inning. We were ahead, 6-4, and a major upset was in the making. The sixth grade's big kicker, Troy, was up.

We were playing pretty deep, but Troy *really* unloaded on this ball. It was a high, deep drive to left field. I started to sprint toward left field, but there was no way I was going to get there. However, our left fielder had a chance. He turned his back to the diamond and ran as hard as he could, looking back over his shoulder at the ball, with his arms stretched out in front of him.

On a playground there are a lot of potentially dangerous pieces of equipment. But nothing is more vicious than the tetherball pole.

I could see everything as I ran toward him. My friend was running right at the pole. He hit it at full speed and bounced off. He stood still for a second—frozen—before he collapsed.

I was really concerned. I ran right over, got the ball, threw it back, and held Troy to a triple.

The point is that my friend wasn't watching where he was going and got hurt big time. I've often wondered why I didn't yell out a word of warning to him. We need to be setting examples for our carnal brothers and sisters and giving them words of warning. If they don't watch where they are going, they're going to get hurt emotionally, spiritually, and physically. They need to see Jesus Christ lived out in our lives as much as non-Christians do.

☐ Spiritual Christians

Spiritual Christians should be your best friends.

"But Jesus spent time with the prostitutes, Pharisees, and tax collectors," you say. That's true, but remember that His closest friends were the disciples. He invested Himself in their lives, and we should do the same.

"Let us consider how we may spur one another on toward love and good deeds" (Hebrews 10:24).

☐ God the Father, Jesus Christ, and the Holy Spirit

Ladies, I want you to conduct a little experiment with me. Go over to a group of guys who are shooting baskets, and just stand at the edge of the court and watch them. You should see a transformation take place in a matter of minutes. They will go from laid-back shooting to intense playing. How come? Because someone is watching them. We usually try harder when someone is watching.

Think back over the past two weeks. What if Jesus Christ had appeared in your room and said, "Hi. I have decided to join you in physical form for the next two weeks. You'll be able to see Me, and your friends will be able to see Me. I'll go everywhere you go, hear everything you say, see everything you do"?

Would the last two weeks have been any different? Would you have gone to the same places? Would you have said anything differently?

I've got news for you: He was and still is right there with you. He sees and hears it all!

Most important is that we set a good example before Jesus Christ. We need to always seek to honor God with our actions, words, and thoughts.

BE KIND

"Be kind and compassionate to one another, forgiving each other, just as in Christ God forgave you" (Ephesians 4:32).

One of the best ways to show kindness is through acts of service. We have a misconception that being a leader means you have to be in front of large crowds and do spectacular things. But that's not true. Kindness shows itself in the little things you do. "If anyone gives even a cup of cold water to one of these little ones because he is my disciple, I tell you the truth, he will certainly not lose his reward" (Matthew 10:42).

Be a cold water server. Imagine being back in Jesus' time on a hot, hot, dusty day. How hard it must have been to find cold water! Today it is easy to get cold water. You just send your little brother to the refrigerator under the threat of a life-ending injury. But back then it had to come from a deep well and be served immediately. For the lucky person who could find it, it was WONDERFUL! We can bring that kind of spiritual and emotional refreshment today to others. "OK, how do I do that?"

- ☐ By sitting with someone who is alone
- ☐ By listening to those who are hurting
- ☐ By writing an encouraging note
- ☐ By helping someone with work that needs to be done
- ☐ By praying with a person in need
- ☐ By reaching out to those who are younger than you

BE A LISTENER

"My dear brothers, take note of this: Everyone should be quick to listen, slow to speak and slow to become angry" (James 1:19).

People say to me, "Greg, I could never be a leader because I'm too shy. I'm not qualified because I'm insecure, because I don't know the Bible well enough, because I look like a gecko, because _____ because _____ because _____" (Fill in the blanks.)

I answer, "Can you listen and show love?" If you say yes, you can be a leader. You may not get up in front of large groups, but you can lead by example.

Andrew the disciple was a behind-the-scenes leader, unlike his brother, Peter, who spoke before the multitudes. Yet both were leaders and important to the Body of Christ. Andrew introduced Peter to Jesus. If it weren't for the Andrews we wouldn't have the Peters.

CONFRONT IN LOVE

"Wounds of a friend can be trusted" (Proverbs 27:6).

When is the last time you wounded a friend? "Greg, I would never wound any of my friends." If you are a true friend you will be willing to wound the people you care about. Let me give you an example.

You are at school Monday morning, and a friend comes up and says, "You should have been at the party Friday night. It was awesome! First, we all got wasted at Tom's. We broke into his parents' liquor cabinet—man, they are going to be so ticked! Then we went over to Kathy's, and everyone started taking off their clothes and jumping into the pool. Kathy was giving out these pills. Couples started getting together. Next thing I know, it is Saturday morning, and I am in bed with this total stranger. You should have been there!"

What's your response? "Oh, that's really funny"?
If you say that, you are totally copping out!

When your friend tells you a story of sin and you say, "That's nice," or just laugh, you are giving your stamp of approval. As long as you go along with it, his conscience is soothed, and he can continue in the same direction.

Do you love your friend enough to confront him and say, "I love you, but what you are doing is wrong"?

When you do that you open the door for the Holy Spirit to work in their lives. Once they know you don't approve, they will have a nagging doubt in the back of their minds that says, *Maybe I shouldn't be doing this. Maybe I should get my life together.*

You may say, "Come on, Greg, who am I to cramp their style? They have to make their own decisions. Who am I to butt in? They'll just get mad at me."

When my son Justin was about two years old, I was holding him in my arms and talking to Bonnie as

she cooked dinner. Bonnie took a pot off the stove and walked over to the sink. The burner on the stove glowed red. Justin looked at that, thought, *How interesting*, and reached out to touch it.

What was my reaction? Did I say, "Hey, who am I to cramp his style? It's his life—who am I to butt in? Justin will just get mad at me anyway. Go ahead, Justin, put your hand on the burner (sizzzzzle). Now put your face on it (sizzle, pop, crackle)"?

No! I turned away as fast as I could, so he couldn't reach it. If I had let him put his hand on that glowing burner, you would have asked, "What kind of a father are you?" And then you would have answered your own question: "Lousy!"

What kind of a friend are you when you silently watch your friends obviously hurting themselves? Lousy!

Yes, they may scream and yell, but that's OK because, chances are, eventually they are going to come back to you and say, "Thanks. You were the only one who loved us enough to confront us."

When you confront your friends make sure that

☐ you have prayed a lot,
☐ you're doing it out of sincere love and concern,
☐ you do it in private (Don't embarrass your friends in front of other people. If you do, they will become bitter toward you, and they won't listen anyway. You will also risk the whole group's turning against you. That will affirm to your friends that they are more cool than you and that what they are doing is OK.),
☐ you are willing to face weaknesses and sin in your own life and that you desire to change.

SET A HIGH MORAL STANDARD

What does it mean to live according to a high moral standard?

> We pray this in order that you may *live a life worthy of the Lord* and may *please him* in every way: *bearing fruit in every good work, growing in the knowledge of God* . . . and *joyfully giving thanks* to the Father. (Colossians 1:10-12)

☐ Live a life worthy of the Lord.
   D. L. Moody said, "It is a great deal better to let God live a holy life through you than to talk about it. Lighthouses do not ring bells and fire cannons to call attention to their shining . . . they just shine." Only in surrendering to Jesus Christ and allowing the Holy Spirit to fill us can we live a life worthy of the Lord.

☐ Please Him.
   Have you ever said, "My goal today is to please God"? You seek to please your boyfriend or girlfriend and your other friends. Why not begin to actively and consciously please God?
   It's never too late to start. You can begin pleasing the Lord right now. Even though you have blown it time after time, you can have a brand-new beginning. Jesus will forgive, cleanse, and empower you so that you can live a life that is pleasing to Him.

☐ Bear fruit in every good work.
   Why doesn't Colossians 1:10 just say, "bearing fruit," instead of "bearing fruit in every good work"? Because you bear fruit in bad works too. "Every good tree bears good fruit, but a bad tree

bears bad fruit. A good tree cannot bear bad fruit, and a bad tree cannot bear good fruit" (Matthew 7:17-18).

What kind of fruit are you bearing? Are people being drawn closer to Christ or driven farther away from Him because of the way you live?

You see, it is a wonderful privilege to be a Christian, but it is also an awesome responsibility. "If anyone causes one of these little ones who believe in me to sin, it would be better for him to have a large millstone hung around his neck and to be drowned in the depths of the sea" (Matthew 18:6). Let me put that verse in today's language.

Let's say my daughter is seventeen, and this guy comes over to take her out on a date.

"You must be Festus. I'm Greg Speck." We shake hands, and I squeeze really hard.

"Come on into the living room. My daughter is still getting ready, but she should be down in

about a week. While we wait, let me tell you something. If you do anything to hurt my daughter physically, emotionally, or spiritually, I have something I want you to do. I will insist that you get into your car and drive to the ocean. When you get there, buy a boat. It doesn't matter how much it costs because you won't be coming back.

"Then I want you to get a millstone—a large, flat stone with a hole in the middle. If you can't find a millstone, any large rock will do. Take a long, strong piece of rope and the rock into the boat with you, and take off. Drive the boat for a few hours until you run out of gas.

"When you look around, you will only be able to see water. There won't be land anywhere nearby. Secure one end of the rope to the rock, and tie the other end around your neck. You'll notice a very hungry, twenty-five-foot great white shark nudging the boat. Throw the rock into the water, and watch it disappear into the dark depths. Feel the jerk on your neck, the ice cold water, and the sense of terror as the great white shark begins to chase you into the depths. Will you drown first or be eaten? Either way, you'll be better off than having to deal with me!"

I pat him on the back and say, "Have a nice time. Oh, by the way, when will you have my daughter back?"

"In about five minutes, sir. I'll just take her out, show her my car, and bring her right back."

You see, that guy would understand that my daughter is very precious to me and that when he is with her he had better behave himself.

That is what God says to us in that verse. It is one thing if you want to go down the tubes, but woe be it unto you if you take someone with you.

So be a leader who bears good fruit. If you aren't, beware—and stay away from my daughters!

☐ Grow in knowledge.

People say, "To be a Christian, you have to commit intellectual suicide because no one with a brain could be a Christian." That is so stupid. There are many facts to back up our faith in Jesus Christ. The more we learn, the stronger our faith will become.

We let other people tell us what our convictions should be. Then someone challenges our faith, and we have no defense. Why? Because we don't think for ourselves. We don't ask hard questions, express doubt, and seek knowledge.

Answer the following questions.

- How do you know there is a God?
- What proof do you have that Jesus Christ was God?
- How do you know the Bible is reliable?
- What evidence do you have that Christ rose from the dead?
- What happens to people who have never heard about Christ when they die?
- Can you still believe in creation even though evolution is taught everywhere?
- Why do good people, babies, and the innocent suffer?

If can't answer these questions, you'd better do some studying, and ask people you respect what they think. But develop your own convictions as you seek what is true and right.

☐ Joyfully give thanks.

One summer a guy named Rick Ragan joined our Royal Servants missions trip. His parents didn't want him to bring his class ring because they were afraid he would lose it. He was determined to bring it, and he assured them he wouldn't lose it. (Famous last words.)

We were at a campsite in Germany when Rick ran up to me with the terrible news—he had lost his ring! He had been throwing a football around, and it must have flown off.

I got all the teens to form a line to look for Rick's ring. We were about sixty across, and we went back and forth, but no ring.

I finally called the group together, and I asked Rick what God was teaching him. He said that God was telling him he needed to listen to his parents. We all prayed and thanked God that the ring was lost and that He was teaching Rick a great lesson. I said we'd look a little longer and see what happened, but we had to leave soon. Less than two minutes later, one of our female staff found the ring.

Thanksgiving releases God to work because when you thank God you are saying, "God, I trust You."

QUOTES

You can preach a better sermon with your life than with your lips.

(Oliver Goldsmith)

A great leader never sets himself above his followers except in carrying responsibilities.

(Jules Ormont)

The great leaders of men in all fields have not been the arrogant and the greedy, but the servants.

(John E. Mitchell)

*I charge you before God that you follow me no
further than you have seen me follow the Lord Jesus
Christ.*

(John Robinson,
    spoken to the pilgrims
    just before they
    boarded the Mayflower
    to sail to America)

10

Do I Need It or Want It?

We tend to dump everything in life together under a "Need" column, instead of distinguishing between our wants and needs.

Here is a pop quiz. Circle the true needs.
I need . . .

1. Someone to care about me
2. A paid vacation to a tropical island
3. A brand-new, bright red Porsche
4. To do something well
5. A group to belong to
6. A lifetime supply of chocolate
7. An acne medicine that works
8. Someone to go to homecoming with
9. Someone to notice when I am doing well
10. My stomach pumped after lunch in the cafeteria
11. The 49'ers to win another Super Bowl
12. A liposuction
13. My date to get a liposuction
14. A new outfit (mine is a week old)
15. To deal with the pain in my life
16. A pit bull
17. The pit bull surgically removed from my leg

If you picked 1, 4, 5, 9, and 15, you were right. Come to think of it, give yourself credit if you picked 17.

You have two sets of values inside you, which I call head and gut values. Head values are what you know *ought* to be important.

☐ God
☐ family
☐ devotions
☐ purity
☐ kindness

Gut values are what we do in pressure situations. The needs in our life usually determine our gut values.

The problem is that often our head and gut values conflict. For example, your head value is purity, but your gut value is a need to be loved. So even though you never thought it would happen, you find yourself involved sexually.

Your head value is family, but your gut value is your desire to fit in to a group. So you are drawn farther and farther away from your family and spend all your time with the group.

You know church is supposed to be important; however, your gut value is to achieve. So you get a job and find yourself working Sundays and Wednesdays, and you don't have time for church anymore.

Your head value says it is good to be kind, but your gut value wants attention and recognition. So you put others down while your friends laugh and think you're great.

Let's look at our basic needs more closely to see if we can better understand why we do what we do.

NEED TO BE LOVED

It is good to need to be loved. But we seek to meet that need in unhealthy ways. We want someone special in our life, someone to care about us. But we run to conditional love that says, "I'll love you if . . ." We have friends who say that they'll love us as long as we dress a certain way, hang around with the right people, and meet their expectations. In conditional dating relationships, your date says, "Sure, I'll love you. Just take off your clothes.

Women fall for this kind of love a lot. Most women I meet are not looking for sex; they are looking for intimacy. They want a guy who will hold and care for them. But the guy isn't interested in that, so she gives herself away sexually to feel a few minutes of love. She isn't looking for the physical pleasure as much as emotional pleasure." Many women do give sex to get love, and many guys play love to get sex.

But the relationship eventually ends, and then she feels worse than she did before. She looks for another relationship that gets physical more quickly. The cycle repeats itself over and over again. The woman goes from relationship to relationship and from bed to bed looking for love but only getting used. After a while she gives up on herself and begins to date loser guys who take advantage of her. But she stays in the relationships—why? Partly because she thinks she doesn't deserves anything better. It's a way for her to punish herself. And partly because deep down inside she is still trying to fulfill that need to be loved.

We need to discover Jesus Christ's unconditional love for us. Christ can meet that need in our lives as no one else can. "I pray that you, being rooted and established in love, may have power, together with all the saints, to grasp how wide and long and high and deep is the love of Christ, and to know this love that surpasses knowledge—that you may be filled to the measure of all the fullness of God" (Ephesians 3:17-19). God loves you right now as much as He has ever loved you in your whole life, and His love is complete.

His love is *not* based on the way you act. He doesn't love you any less if you sin, or any more if you read your Bible and pray. HE JUST LOVES YOU!

NEED TO BELONG

I was speaking at a Christian high school, and a beautiful girl came up to me. She was a junior, and she said, "Greg, I go to all the parties, and I'm in the popular group. But I'm so lonely." She began to weep and then added, "I just feel so empty inside."

Our need to be accepted is very strong. Either verbally or subconsciously we say to our friends, "If you'll accept me and help me fit in I'll do ANYTHING." Then we do things we don't want to do, don't like doing, and are ashamed of.

That's why a breakup can be such a devastating experience. When you break up, you not only lose that person whom you love; you also lose your sense of belonging. Sometimes you even lose the gang you've been hanging around with. A deep pain and emptiness takes over. You panic and rush around trying to find someone else to date. See how easily the need to belong can lead to compromise and sin?

Jesus Christ can fulfill your need to belong. "Now you are the body of Christ, and each one of you is a part of it" (1 Corinthians 12:27). In Jesus Christ you belong to His Body. It doesn't matter if you are . . .

> rich or poor
> heavy or skinny
> beautiful or Greg Speck (people think I look like
>   a combination of Winnie-the-Pooh, Fred Flin-
>   stone, and Moe on the Three Stooges)
> dating or not
> passing or flunking
> athletic or Pee Wee Herman

We are all united in Christ. Once we commit ourselves to Christ we become part of a family that stretch-
es throughout the world.

You are a child of God, and He promises, "Never
will I leave you; never will I forsake you" (Hebrews
13:5). Boyfriends may drop you, girlfriends leave you,
and friends reject you, but Jesus Christ will always
love and care for you.

NEED TO ACHIEVE AND BE RECOGNIZED FOR MY ACHIEVEMENTS

We all need to be able to do something that brings
us fulfillment. But things are happening so fast all
around us that at times we feel totally out of control.
The family is pulling apart, work's a hassle, there's
pressure from school, the uncertain future, shallow
relationships—AHHHH! It seems that no matter what I
try to do, I screw up. Nobody notices when I do well,

but everyone points out when I blow it. So I say, "If I can't achieve in positive ways, I'll seek to achieve in negative ways." The emptiness deep inside won't go away, so I say, "OK, I'll fill it by:

- ☐ going to parties
- ☐ seeking boyfriends or girlfriends
- ☐ striving for the perfect body
- ☐ accumulating things
- ☐ having sex
- ☐ using drugs
- ☐ drinking

But I'm still miserable. So what's the answer?

Jesus Christ is sufficient to meet this need, too. Your unique gifts, talents, and abilities are an important part of the Body of Christ. He wants to use you for great things!

You do not have to achieve, plan, or plot to get attention. Humble yourself before God, and He will lift you up. As God works through your life, others will notice.

NEED TO DEAL WITH PAIN

When you look at your life, God reveals pain from your past. You try to deal with it, saying, "I can handle it. I don't need anyone else." That works for a while, but something brings back the hurtful memories, and the pain raises its ugly head again.

You need to let Jesus heal you through others. God brings healing through the Body of Christ. "We who are strong ought to bear with the failings of the weak and not to please ourselves" (Romans 15:1). All of us are weak in certain areas and at certain times, so we need to allow others to support and help us.

Find someone you can trust, and tell him or her about your pain. "Confess your sins to each other and pray for each other so that you may be healed" (James 5:16). When you confess your sin and pain to others, God will bring healing. And you will have righteous individuals praying for you.

Don't ignore your pain anymore. God wants to turn your open wounds into scars. When you have an open wound you are totally preoccupied with it. But as it heals, it becomes a scar. It may still demand attention, but as time goes by you think about it less and less.

You have needs, and that's OK. The question is, How are you seeking to fulfill them? Look to the Person of Jesus Christ and the Body of Christ to meet your needs. When you do, you'll be satisfied, joyful, and at peace.

"Peace I leave with you; my peace I give you. I do not give to you as the world gives. Do not let your hearts be troubled and do not be afraid" (John 14:27).

QUOTES

When you have nothing left but God, then for the first time you become aware that God is enough.

(Maude Royden)

It is difficult to make a man miserable who claims kindred to the great God who made him.

(Abraham Lincoln)

An infinite God can give all of Himself to each of His children as fully as if there were no others.

(A. W. Tozer)

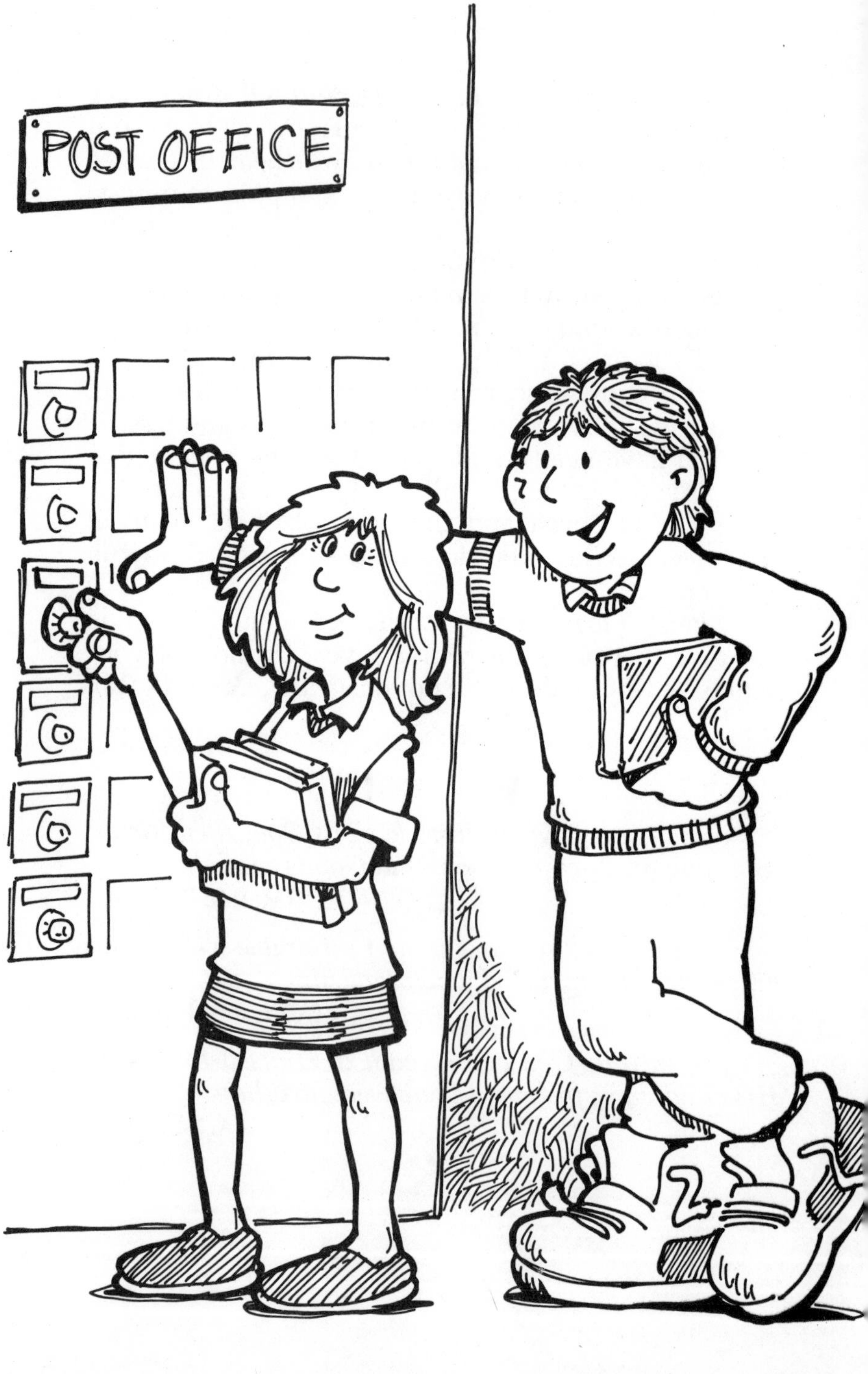
POST OFFICE

11

Peer Pressure—The Heat's On!

Let's say you're a freshman at a state university. You're starting to get settled, and your roommate is OK, but you haven't made many friends, and you're feeling pretty lonely.

One afternoon you are getting the mail out of your P.O. box when a senior walks up to you. He begins to joke around with you, and he seems to be a really nice guy. He tells you about a party at his frat house and invites you to come. You're shocked! When you recover you thank him profusely and tell him you wouldn't miss it.

The night of the party arrives, and you show up at the frat house. The party is in full swing as the same guy meets you at the door. He takes you around, introducing you to everyone.

It dawns on you that you are the only underclassman. You'd be pretty intimidated if everyone wasn't being so friendly and kind.

You've been there for about two hours, having a great time, when the senior invites you to come down into the basement with him. You join a group of people who are talking, laughing, and listening to some tunes.

Then the senior pulls out a funny-looking cigarette and lights it. He takes a hit and passes it to the person next to him. All of a sudden you realize, *Hey! That isn't a cigarette—it's marag—I mean, marju—morge —marrigegn—it's grass!*

149

Now, what are you going to do? Initially you think, *Well, not everyone will take a hit.* But everyone does, and as it gets closer to you, the pressure builds. You are a freshman among juniors and seniors who have befriended you. What are you going to do?

It's two people away from you. What now?

The guy next to you takes a deep drag. You can almost hear your heart pounding, and you feel the sweat running down your face. He hands you the joint —everyone is talking and laughing, but they are also watching you. *What are you going to do?*

Maybe you say, "I'll just do it this one time. I won't do it again, but I don't want to look like a total geek. I'll take one hit, but then I won't do it anymore, I promise."

GOTCHA! If Satan can get you to compromise once, it will be much easier the second time. The third time won't be tough at all, and you'll hardly think about it the fourth. Pretty soon you'll be doing things regularly that six months ago you swore you would never do.

What happens when you give in to negative peer pressure? You lose your identity in three stages.

1. *Who am I?*

You begin to question yourself and your faith. Who am I really? Do I really believe in God? Do I buy into all the things my parents have been telling me?

We fool ourselves by saying, "I'm my own person, doing my own thing." We say we want to experience life for ourselves, so we get involved in things we know are wrong. But in reality, other people are having a huge impact on our life. Our peers are shaping our thoughts, activities, and choices. We need to gain their approval and shun their disapproval so fiercely that we stop thinking through the choices we make and just go with the flow. God seems far away. In time, we move to stage 2.

2. *I'm nobody.*

One day you take a good look at yourself, and you think, *What am I doing?* You feel terrible about all the things you have been doing. At this point you are at a crossroad. Either you turn around and get your life back together, or you move on to stage 3.

3. *It doesn't matter anymore.*

"I've already gone this far. I've done so much that it doesn't matter now." You give up on yourself and dive headfirst into sin. You have now completely lost your identity and purpose for living. Your only hope is the love and forgiveness of Jesus Christ. You can still get it back together, but it's tough because you have become so hardened toward the things of God.

What is negative peer pressure? It's allowing people to talk you into doing things that you don't want to do or shouldn't be doing. What are some areas you feel pressured in right now?

SEX

There is a lot of pressure today to get involved sexually. The fact is, in the long run premarital sex is going to cause you more emotional and spiritual pain than it will give you physical pleasure. You *can* show self-control. You don't have to give up or give in. Virginity is something to be proud of!

Many guys feel pressured to have sex, just to prove that they are really men. That is so stupid! It does not prove that you are a man. If intercourse proved that you were a real man then dogs, hippos, cats, and bears could be classified as real men!

Look to God. "The body is not meant for sexual immorality, but for the Lord, and the Lord for the body. . . . Flee from sexual immorality. All other sins a man commits are outside his body, but he who sins sexually sins against his own body. Do you not know that your body is a temple of the Holy Spirit, who is in you, whom you have received from God?" (1 Corinthians 6:13, 18-19).

ALCOHOL AND DRUGS

You have seen the programs, and you have read the articles about the dangers of substance abuse. People never mean to become alcoholics or addicts, but it happens.

Don't be pressured into doing things that have the potential to control you and even kill you. Drunk driving and overdosing are two prime examples. Use your brain!

Look to God. "Let us behave decently, as in the daytime, not in orgies and drunkenness, not in sexual immorality and debauchery, not in dissension and jealousy. Rather, clothe yourselves with the Lord Jesus Christ, and do not think about how to gratify the desires of the sinful nature" (Romans 13:13-14).

STUFF

The world is always pressuring us to possess more things. But no matter how much you buy, you never, ever arrive. Have you noticed that you never go to your closet and say, "There. I have everything I need to be stylish." Why not? Because the world says, "Did you think that outfit was in? Oh, that was last week." They keep changing the styles because they want your money.

Let's say you want a pet. And the pet you want more than anything is a donkey. When you get it, you decide to play a game with it.

You take a stick, and tie a piece of string to one end. Then tie a carrot to the other end of the string. Get on the donkey's back, and hold the stick over its head so the carrot hangs down in front of its face. *The donkey will begin to chase the carrot, thinking, Oh boy, oh boy, oh boy. I'm going to get a carrot, I'm going to get a carrot.* All day long it will chase that carrot, but it never, ever gets to it.

Some individuals are like that. They chase after the world and its cars, stereos, gadgets, and gimmicks. But even when they get that stuff, they haven't arrived because they're still empty inside.

Look to God. "I know what it is to be in need, and I know what it is to have plenty. I have learned the secret of being content in any and every situation, wheth-

er well fed or hungry, whether living in plenty or in want" (Philippians 4:12).

PHYSICAL APPEARANCE

Our society says that the ultimate is having a perfect body, shining hair, clear complexion, and bright, white teeth. Some of us pursue that perfect image. Maybe we starve ourselves and become anorexic, or we binge and throw up. Maybe we cause our body great damage by taking steroids so we can look good. Even after we endure hours of aerobics, weight lifting, running, and dieting to make ourselves slim and trim, we find that our happiness is fleeting, at best.

Now don't get me wrong. We need to take care of our bodies. But that can't become the driving force of our life. If we spent half as much time working on our inside as we do on our outside we wouldn't have as many problems as we do!

Sometimes I meet a woman and my initial reaction is *Wow, she's good looking.* But after I spend some time talking to her, her beauty fades because she is empty inside. I'll meet another woman and think, *Well, she's OK looking.* But after talking a while, her beauty grows because on the inside she is beautiful.

Remember, beauty is totally subjective. Each of us has his own standard. For some individuals you will be one of the most beautiful people alive. You don't have to turn into someone you aren't. You can be yourself!

Look to God. "The Lord does not look at the things man looks at. Man looks at the outward appearance, but the Lord looks at the heart'" (1 Samuel 16:7).

God tells us how to deal with peer pressure. "Do not conform any longer to the pattern of this world,

but be transformed by the renewing of your mind"
(Romans 12:2).

☐ "Do not conform any longer to the pattern of this
world." Why does God say that? Is it because He's
a killjoy and wants to rob you of excitement and
fun? No! It's because He knows that the world
doesn't give a rip about you. All the world cares
about is that everyone act, dress, and smell alike.
☐ "Be transformed." That means become different.
You say, "I don't like who I am, what I'm doing, or
who I am becoming. Greg, I want to be different,
but how do I do it?"
☐ "By the renewing of your mind." The transformation begins when you know God's truth and act
upon it.

Let's learn God's truth about peer pressure. As
we apply it to our lives, peer pressure will have less
and less of a hold on us. What is the truth God wants
us to know?

THINK ABOUT TOMORROW

Much of what is important to us right now won't
matter at all five years from now. Think back five
years ago . . .

    ☐ What were the styles?
    ☐ What things did you do?
    ☐ What did you think was fun?
    ☐ Who were your friends?

The things you did and the stuff you collected
then probably has little appeal now. In five years, you
won't be caught dead in some of the things you wear
now.

You may be in love now, but will your girlfriend or boyfriend still be around in five years? Probably not. Don't do anything that you will regret in five years such as giving away your virginity.

You could set every sport record at your high school, graduate, and go back five years later. You would strut onto campus and say, "Hi!"

People would say, "Who are you?"

"Who am I! See all those plaques, trophies, ribbons, and awards? I won those!" Not many people are going to care. You see, that was five years ago, and they are more interested in the present.

Here is a little test. No fair cheating and looking up the answers. See how many you know from memory.

Who won

☐ the Super Bowl four years ago?
☐ the Miss America pageant two years ago?

☐ the Indianapolis 500 one year ago?
☐ the World Series five years ago?
☐ homecoming queen five years ago?
☐ *Time*'s Man of the Year two years ago?
☐ *Sports Illustrated*'s Athlete of the Year four years ago?

You could become Miss Universe, Miss America, Miss Iowa, Miss Des Moines, or Miss Corn Cobb, but in five years few people will remember or care.

Besides God and family, the things that are important now probably won't be important in a few years. "The world and its desires pass away, but the man who does the will of God lives forever" (1 John 2:17).

LOOK AT PEOPLE FROM GOD'S POINT OF VIEW

Do you know what the root of peer pressure is? Fear! We are afraid of what other people think, so we give in to the peer pressure.

A three-step sequence takes place here.

1. We fear men.
2. So we follow them. We do whatever it takes to get them to like us.
3. Then we are snared in the trap of peer pressure. We do and say things that we would never have done or said on our own.

The good news is that the more we see people from God's point of view, the less likely we are to fear them. People are small and weak in God's eyes. God kind of looks at us as we look at ants. It's hard to imagine being pressured into something by an ant.

"Please don't laugh at me, Mr. Ant. All right, all right, I'll do it, but please, don't hurt me, don't mock me, Mr. Ant. If I do this, can I sit on your anthill with you and smoke some grasshoppers?" That would be pretty stupid. But that's how we sound when we fear other people.

What's the worst thing man can do to you? He can only kill you! Some of you are thinking, *Excuse me, but I think that is kind of bad.* But don't forget that to live is Christ and to die is gain. If you are a Christian and someone kills you, you go to heaven.

"I tell you, my friends, do not be afraid of those who kill the body and after that can do no more. But I will show you whom you should fear: Fear him who, after the killing of the body, has power to throw you into hell" (Luke 12:4-5). Instead of being scared of man, we should fear God because He decides where we will spend eternity. To fear God is to respect Him enough to stop doing what's wrong and start doing what's right.

When you finally decide to fear God you'll realize that you no longer need to fear man. Not only is God more powerful than man, but He is also on your side and will protect you. "Are not five sparrows sold for two pennies? Yet not one of them is forgotten by God. Indeed, the very hairs of your head are all numbered. Don't be afraid; you are worth more than many sparrows" (Luke 12:6-7; see Isaiah 51:12-13, 15).

I went back for my high school reunion, and I was amazed. I saw all those people I used to be afraid of. Now they were old and bald, fat and messed up, jobless, and divorced. I looked at them and thought, *Wow, I can't believe that I used to be intimidated by these people.*

They're only people, not gods. There is only one God! The people who scare you have problems and hurts just like everyone else.

Compare Your Life to Eternity

How long are you going to live? Some of us could live to be 70 easily. Maybe even 100. Will you live to be 120? It's doubtful. 150? NO!

Now how long is eternity?

Take a solid granite block one hundred miles long, one hundred miles wide, and one hundred miles high. Now encase it in a huge dome, so it isn't affected by weather. Take a parakeet to that dome, open the door, and let the parakeet in to sharpen its beak on the granite block for ten seconds.

After ten seconds, take the bird and leave. Wait one thousand years, then let the little bird sharpen its beak for ten seconds, and then depart. Keep doing that at one-thousand-year intervals.

When that parakeet has finally worn that block down to nothing, one moment will have passed in

eternity. What is your life compared to that? "Why, you do not even know what will happen tomorrow. What is your life? You are a mist that appears for a little while and then vanishes" (James 4:14).

So when you follow the crowd, give in to peer pressure, and choose to screw up for one hundred years, you are throwing away eternity in exchange for a few years of "fun." That's stupid!

Let's say I'm going to give you $1 billion, tax-free, but there's a catch. You have to resist peer pressure for the next thirty days.

Could you do it? YES! Why? Because you realize that what you'll get at the end of the thirty days is far better than the rewards of giving in to pressure.

If I brought you several good-looking members of the opposite sex and said, "Here, you can sleep with any one of them. Take your pick," you would say, "Forget it. In one short month I'm going to get a billion dollars."

What if I brought you some alcohol and drugs and said, "It's all for you. Have some. If you don't, you'll look like a total nerd"? You would say, "Get that stuff out of my face. I don't need it, because in one short month I'm going to get a billion dollars."

"Come on, if you don't do what we say, we'll laugh at you, put you down, tell lies about you, and gossip."

"Go ahead, laugh at me. I don't care, because in one short month I'm going to get a billion dollars."

The benefits of inheriting $1 billion far outweigh the persecution that you would have to put up with. So when the world pressures you to do things that you know are wrong, say, "Forget it. In one short life-time I'm going to inherit all of heaven." The glory and wonder of heaven are far more valuable than a billion dollars!

Are you going to blow God off, give in to peer pressure for the next seventy years, and go to hell? "What good is it for a man to gain the whole world, yet forfeit his soul?" (Mark 8:36). Or are you going to trust God, follow Him, and gain the reward that's waiting for you?

Bad company is going to bring you down (1 Corinthians 15:33). So make your closest friends people who truly love Jesus Christ. Then you can begin to exert some positive peer pressure. You see, peer pressure isn't bad if we are seeking to impact others positively.

Friday night rolls around, and your friends are going to a party. Why? Because everyone else is, and they don't know what else to do. So you and your Christian friends come up with some creative alternatives. Of all people, Christians ought to know how to have a good time without getting involved in sin.

You can be wild and crazy as a youth group, or just a few of you can get together. People are looking for a good excuse not to go to the parties. Realistically, some "party heads" won't be interested in any other activities, no matter how much fun they are. Their idea of having fun is getting drunk and spending the evening with their heads in the toilet. (Sounds like a blast, huh?) Begin to exert some positive peer pressure by giving your friends some creative alternatives. By giving your friends other options for their Friday nights, you are giving them some positive alternatives.

We started this chapter at the frat party. They just handed you a joint. What are you going to do?

Take the joint, and pass it on. You'll probably get a reaction. There is usually at least one big mouth who has to point that out to everyone.

He (or she) will probably say, "Hey, what's the matter with you? How come you didn't take a hit?"

Simply say, "Because I choose not to."

That probably won't satisfy him. "Come on, everybody is doing it. Don't be stupid."

As lovingly as possible say, "Look, I haven't hassled you because you are doing it. Don't get on my back because I'm not."

You know what you'll discover? Your friends will allow you to be you. If they don't like you because you won't smoke, drink, swear, steal, cheat, take off your clothes, and otherwise meet their expectations, then they don't like you period. You might as well find that out early in the relationship, so you can find some other friends.

Don't let negative peer pressure lead you down the tubes. Show some courage, and exert some positive peer pressure. God might begin to use you, and you might start coming alive!

QUOTES

I am only one, but I am one. I can't do everything, but I can do something. And what I can do, that I ought to do. And what I ought to do, by the grace of God, I shall do.

(Edward E. Hale)

Peer pressure is a cow pie.

(Pat Hurley)

Learn to say no; it will be of more use to you than to be able to read Latin.

(Charles Spurgeon)

12

Satan—Alive and Well . . . and a Loser

It was a Sunday at about 10:30 P.M. The phone rang. I immediately recognized the caller as a member from our church.

"Greg, can you come over to our house?"

"Yeah, sure. What's the problem?"

"Well, we have a young man here, and we believe he is demon-possessed. We'd like you to come over and talk with him."

I said, "Oh, OK." I hung up the phone, and my initial reaction was, *Why me?* I was an associate pastor and minister to youth at a church in Rockford, Illinois, and I said, *God, why me? There are three other pastors on staff—I mean, I'm just the youth guy. Why'd they call me?*

It was as if God answered, "Greg, I want to use you."

I went into my room, got down on my knees, and said, "God, I have no idea what I'm doing. I've never dealt with this before. I don't know what to say, and I don't know how to act. God, You're going to have to help me."

I picked up my Bible, got into the car, and drove over to the church member's home. I rang the doorbell, and they brought me into the living room. It was like walking into a different world.

The lights were all dimmed, and the furniture had all been pushed back against the wall, so there was a big open spot in the middle of the room. In the center of the room was a young man around twenty years old. I'll say his name was Dave. He was down on all fours making animal sounds and growling. I said, "What happened here?"

The church member said, "The doorbell rang. I opened the door, and this young man was standing there. His face, arms, and hands were covered with blood. I thought he had been in an accident, so we brought him into the house and began to clean him up.

"Then we noticed that there were no cuts, no place the blood was coming from. We asked him what had happened, and he told us that he had made a sacrifice to Satan. He had taken a cat or a dog, cut it open, emptied out the blood, and smeared it over his face and arms. We tried to talk to him about the Lord, and he went crazy. He went wild, flopped down in the middle of the room, and hasn't moved since."

Whoa. I walked over and stood in front of him. I put my hand on his shoulder to get his attention, but he reared up, screamed, and began to throw punches. We were only a foot apart, so I ducked and brought up my left hand to protect myself because I knew I was about to get fagged. But all of a sudden, I realized that none of his punches were landing. His eyes were closed, and we were at point-blank range, yet every punch missed me.

We began to deal with the demons that were controlling his life. Amazing things happened that night. Dave kept trying to hurt himself. He'd run over to a table and smash his head into it. He'd pick up knick-knacks and try to cut himself. Finally, we had to pin him down on the floor. He had incredible strength, and it took four men to hold him. Finally, after hours of warfare, I prayed and commanded the demon to leave in the name of Jesus Christ.

Dave had a ring that looked like a cheap dime store ring. It had a black stone in it, and if you held the stone in a certain way, it looked as if a little face were carved in the stone. Dave said it was his satanic ring. He said if I took it, I would take his life. I thought, *Great!*—and took the ring.

I went back to my place with the ring. I thought, *Won't this be great? I can go on speaking engagements and bring the ring with me. When I talk about the occult, I can pass around the ring. The people in the crowd will be able to hold it.*

But God said, "Wrong, Greg. Get rid of the ring." So I went outside, put the ring down on the street, prayed over it, giving it to the Lord, and hit it with a hammer. It shattered into a thousand pieces.

I had the next day off—a nice, relaxing day. That evening at about 10:00 the phone rang.

A polite voice said, "Is this Greg Speck?" He sounded like a man in his forties.

I said, "Yes, it is."

"Do you know Dave So-and-so?"

"Yes, I do."

"Did you take a ring from him last night?"

"Yes."

The voice said, "Mr. Speck, we're going to have to have the ring back."

"Excuse me, but who is 'we'?" I asked.

The man identified himself as a member of Rockford's Church of Satan. I had never known that Rockford even had a church of Satan. I said, "Listen, I don't have the ring. I destroyed it."

The man said, "Well then, Mr. Speck, you're going to have to gain forgiveness. We'll come over to your place this evening with a bowl of blood. We want you to dip your hands in the blood and say these words—" I can't say what the words were because they were totally nonsensical. Yet I had the feeling that they meant something.

I said, "No way. There's no way I'm going to wash my hands in any blood."

There was a pause, and he said, "I guess we'll just have to wreck your church." Then he hung up.

I thought, *Give me a break. Tomorrow Pastor is going to show up at church and see the windows smashed out, blood splashed all over the walls, the pews destroyed, the pulpit knocked over—everything destroyed —and he's going to look around and say, "WHO'S RE-SPONSIBLE FOR THIS?"*

It was about 11:30 P.M. by then, but I decided to call my pastor.

"Hi, Pastor. This is your little buddy Greg. Listen, I have some news for you." I told him everything that had happened and that the Church of Satan was going to come to our church to destroy it. Then I asked him if he wanted my resignation.

He said, "No way. In fact, that's tremendous! Tell them to destroy the church. We'll call in the news media and expose the fact that a group like that is working in Rockford. That's great, Greg, good job."

"Huh? Oh sure, I knew it all the time. OK, thanks." I was trying to decide whether or not to go bed, but at midnight the phone rang again.

Same voice: "Mr. Speck, we need the ring returned."

I felt like saying, "Read my lips," but I just repeated, "I don't have the ring, and even if I did I wouldn't give it to you."

"Then you are going to have to gain forgiveness."

"I'm not interested in gaining forgiveness from you. I'm not going to wash my hands in any blood."

He said, "Do you have a Bible?"

What! "Yes, I have a Bible."

"Would you open it to the book of Leviticus?"

This should be good. Satan is going to try to use Scripture.

"Now read Leviticus 4:3-6."

"'If the anointed priest sins, bringing guilt on the people, he must bring to the Lord a young bull without defect as a sin offering for the sin he has committed. He is to present the bull at the entrance to the Tent of Meeting before the Lord. He is to lay his hand on its head and slaughter it before the Lord. Then the anointed priest shall take some of the bull's blood and carry it into the Tent of Meeting. He is to dip his finger into the blood and sprinkle some of it seven times before the Lord, in front of the curtain of the sanctuary.'"

He said, "See, Mr. Speck, they made blood offerings back in the Old Testament. That's all we are asking you to do." Then he said something that Satan has whispered to me hundreds of times, but it was the first time I'd heard him say it out loud. "Besides, Mr. Speck, who would know? It's the middle of the night. We won't tell anybody, you certainly won't tell anybody—hey, nobody will know."

I remembered Hebrews 13:4: "Nothing in all creation is hidden from God's sight. Everything is uncovered and laid bare before the eyes of him to whom we must give an account." I said, "Wait a second, the two most important individuals are going to see everything I do. First, God is going to see it. Second, I would see it, and I'm not going to do it. Besides, the Bible is talking about making a blood offering to God, and you want me to make a sacrifice to Satan. It's not the same thing at all. Do you have a Bible?"

"Well, yes."

"I want you to turn to the book of Isaiah. Go back to your leader, and read her two passages of Scripture. The first I claim for myself. Isaiah 41:11: 'All who rage against you will surely be ashamed and disgraced; those who oppose you will be as nothing and perish.'

"Second, read her verses 21-24. Tell her that these verses apply to her: '"Present your case," says the Lord. "Set forth your arguments," says Jacob's King. "Bring in your idols to tell us what is going to happen. . . . Tell us what the future holds, so we may know that you are gods. Do something, whether good or bad, so that we will be dismayed and filled with fear. But you are less than nothing and your works are utterly worthless; he who chooses you is detestable."'"

"Whoa, I can't tell her that."

"Tell her that Greg Speck says those verses describe her."

He hung up.

I sat there, and I waited. At 1:30 the phone rang. I wanted to say, "Hello, Wong Tong Laundry. You got wrong number." But I didn't.

Same voice: "Mr. Speck?"

"Yes."

"Mr. Speck, our leader is in a rage. Anytime your name is mentioned she goes crazy and begins to curse. Greg, I'm really becoming fearful for your life—"

Sure, I'll bet you are really concerned.

"—and I want you to know, Greg, that we are going to have to have the ring back."

"I DON'T HAVE THE RING! The ring is destroyed, and even if I had it, I would not give it to you."

"Then you are going to have to wash your hands in the blood."

"No, I'm not going to wash my hands in blood. I'm not interested in gaining forgiveness from you."

"You have two options: Return the ring, or wash your hands in the blood."

I said, "Wrong! I have option number three, which is to reject options one and two. I choose option number three!"

"Mr. Speck, I doubt very seriously that you will see tomorrow morning." And he hung up the phone.

I don't know if your life has ever been threatened, but I will never forget that threat as long as I live. I held the phone up to my ear for a second, thinking, *I'm in big trouble. Wait a second, come back here! Give me the operator, give me the marines, give me somebody!*

I finally put the phone back in the cradle. *What am I going to do? I know, I'll leave! I'll get out of here . . . Oh, wait. I can't do that. They'll come in and trash my place . . .*

I'll call the police. That's what I'll do. Hmm, that will sound good. I'll tell them the whole story, and they'll say, "What kind of drugs are you doing, son?" No, I can't to do that . . .

I know! I'll wait here until I hear them coming. Then I'll run and call the police, jump out the window, get away, and the police will come and arrest them. Whoopeee—I win!

There I was, this great man of God, really trusting Jesus Christ. I went around the house and turned on every light. Fully dressed with even my shoes on, I laid down in bed. I laid there completely alert, with every muscle tensed.

God finally suggested that I read my Bible. I had been doing my devotions in Isaiah, so I turned to chapter 50 and read it. But it went in one ear and out the other. I started reading chapter 51, half reading and half listening for noises. Nothing was sinking in, but all of a sudden I got to verse 12, and God slapped me across the face.

I, even I, am he who comforts you. Who are you
that you fear mortal men, the sons of men, who are
but grass, that you forget the Lord your Maker, who
stretched out the heavens and laid the foundations
of the earth, that you live in constant terror every
day because of the wrath of the oppressor, who is
bent on destruction? . . . For I am the Lord your
God, who churns up the sea so that its waves roar—
the Lord Almighty is his name. I have put my words
in your mouth and covered you with the shadow of
my hand. (vv. 12-16)

The tears began to roll down my face. I realized
that God had been with me through the whole thing.
He had put the words in my mouth and covered me
with the shadow of His hand. Nobody was going to
harm me. I put on my jammies, got into bed, and
turned off the light. But I was thinking, *Lord I just
really don't know if I can get to slee—zzzzz.*

All of a sudden my alarm clock was going off. It was morning! The sun was shining, the birds were singing, and I was alive! I felt great!

I had a good day at work. That evening at about 11:30 the phone rang. I thought, *I don't believe this. They're calling for directions to my house.*

The same voice said, "Mr. Speck, we have made a decision."

"All right."

"Mr. Speck, we have decided to forgive you."

I stood there in silence for a few seconds. Then I started to laugh. "With all your power, with all your strength, with all your might, you couldn't even touch me, could you?"

"I just wanted you to know that you are forgiven."

"Listen, I want you to go to your leader and tell her that I want to meet with her."

"Ha, there is no way she will do that."

"Do you know why? Because she is a second-rate power. The real power, the real strength is in the Person of Jesus Christ."

"Well, that's all I wanted to tell you."

I never heard from the Church of Satan in Rockford again. Yes, Satan is alive and well—but he is a loser.

You think your battle is against your parents, but you're wrong. You think your battle is against your teachers, but it's not. You've been rebelling against the wrong individuals. You need to rebel against Satan because your fight is not against flesh and blood; it's against the spiritual forces of evil.

In Satan we face a very strong foe. He literally hates God and His followers, so he constantly plots against Christians to bring us down. Satan is good at what he does. Do you know why? Because he's had a lot of practice. You see, Satan has had more than six thousand years to do what he does.

Satan desires two basic things from us:

☐ He wants us to fear him.

Satan feeds on fear, and if he can get us to be afraid, then he can remove our focus from God. He uses fear to manipulate us. We should never, ever fear Satan. We need to stay away from things that cause fear, such as stupid movies—*Nightmare on Elm Street, Part 40—Freddie Slashes the Little Mermaid.*

It *really* bothers me when Christian organizations participate in haunted houses during Halloween. Halloween is Satan's high holiday and is as important to him as Christmas or Easter is to us. You don't see Satan setting up little nativity scenes during Christmas. Instead of taking part in his season, we ought to be praying against him. We are at war, and we need to stay away from the things that cause fear.

☐ He wants us to worship him.

He wants us to fall to our knees and worship him as lord Satan. Satanic services are times to worship Satan, which bring him honor and disgrace to God. To worship Satan is a sick thing to do. When you do that, you are worshiping evil. Remember that when you worship Satan, you are also acknowledging that there is a God and you stand opposed to Him.

Let's check out Satan's beginning. Genesis 1:1 says that God created the heavens and the earth. As part of this creation, God brought into existence beings called angels. "By him all things were created:

things in heaven and on earth, visible and invisible, whether thrones or powers or rulers or authorities; all things were created by him and for him" (Colossians 1:16). One angel especially stood out. His name was Lucifer, which means bright and shining one.

Lucifer was God's creation, but he rebelled against God. Lucifer said in his heart, "I will ascend to heaven; I will raise my throne above the stars of God; I will sit enthroned on the mount of assembly, on the utmost heights of the sacred mountain. I will ascend above the tops of the clouds; I will make myself like the Most High" (Isaiah 14:13-14).

Lucifer wanted his own will. He was unwilling to humble himself before God. In other words, Lucifer was conceited (1 Timothy 3:6).

Lucifer thought he was going to be like God. The New Age movement and other cults tell us we are gods. Who do you think is behind those groups?

Swift judgment followed Lucifer's rebellion, and he was cast down from his important position in heaven to earth. He became Satan, which means adversary. There was also a group of angels whom Satan deceived into rebelling with him. They were also cast down, and they are now his demons. "And there was war in heaven. Michael and his angels fought against the dragon, and the dragon and his angels fought back. But he was not strong enough, and they lost their place in heaven. The great dragon was hurled down— that ancient serpent called the devil or Satan, who leads the whole world astray. He was hurled to earth, and his angels with him" (Revelation 12:7-9).

Today we are involved in warfare with Satan. It should not surprise Christians that we have problems, temptations, and suffering. As a matter of fact, it ought to surprise and bother us if we are *not* under attack. When we commit our lives to Jesus Christ and

follow Him, we better expect to be opposed because
we have an adversary in Satan.

He is doomed, and he knows it. But he wants to
take as many with him as possible. When you became
a Christian, he lost you, so why does he still bother
with you?

☐ Because he is mad at you and wants you to be miserable. That makes him happy.
☐ He doesn't want you to lead anyone else to Christ.
  He wants you to take your focus off Christ and become apathetic and carnal. When that happens
  you become such a lousy example that Satan uses
  you to keep others away from Christ. We hear proof
  of that when we hear non-Christians say, "I know
  some Christians, and they don't act any differently
  than I do. What's the big deal about becoming a
  Christian?"

We have to wake up! There is a battle raging
around us. People are dying and going to hell, but
we're more concerned about looking good and getting
a date. How can we prepare ourselves for the attacks
and fight back?

Ephesians 6:10-18 is a great passage about spiritual warfare. Let's look at what it says in detail.

"BE STRONG IN THE LORD AND IN HIS MIGHTY POWER"

Do you realize that Satan's power and wisdom
are second only to that of God the Father, Jesus Christ,
and the Holy Spirit? Satan is not to be taken lightly.
Many godly men and women throughout the ages have
been seriously wounded by him.

When we are involved in spiritual warfare—
which is almost all the time—we can't win in our own
strength. It's not enough to have determination and
good intentions. We will never ever be strong enough
on our own. Our strength comes from the Lord. Ask
the Holy Spirit to fill you with His power, and surrender control of your life to Him.

"AGAINST THE DEVIL'S SCHEMES"

We have a crafty and powerful adversary. Don't
underestimate him. When you say, "Hey, nobody
runs my life. I make my own decisions." Satan just
sits back and smiles. When you rebel against your
parents and God, you become easy prey for the devil.
Satan isn't compared to a dragon and a lion just for
fun. He is powerful.

But don't overestimate Satan's power either.
Yes, he is powerful and cunning, but when you are
committed to Jesus Christ, you can claim 1 John 4:4:
"You, dear children, are from God and have overcome them, because the one who is in you is greater
than the one who is in the world."

"WHEN THE DAY OF EVIL COMES, YOU MAY BE ABLE TO STAND YOUR GROUND"

Notice that it doesn't say, "*If* the day of evil
comes." It says *when.* We are going to be attacked,
and we had better be prepared. When you are at war,
you have to be prepared for attack at all times. The
enemy is not going to let you know when he is coming. He wants to totally surprise you.

So it's important that we wear our armor every
day. Then when temptations come, you'll be able to
stand your ground. When the battle is over and the

smoke has cleared, you'll still be standing firm because you are armed and empowered by the Holy Spirit.

"WITH THE BELT OF TRUTH"

It's pretty hard to fight while you're trying to hold your pants up. The belt holds all the other pieces of armor together. Your belt holds your sword, one of your offensive weapons. Without the belt, your armor is in jeopardy. Put another way, you would be in trouble!

What does the belt symbolize? Truth. The foundation of the armor is truth, which means two things.

☐ It means that you understand the truth about God. You know who He is. You understand your birthright and who you are in Christ.

☐ It also means that you have integrity and that you tell the truth. Some of you are first-class liars. When you lie, you are being attacked and defeated by Satan. Never, ever, ever lie! Why? Because then your word doesn't mean anything, and you don't mean anything.When you lie, you speak Satan's native tongue.

"WITH THE BREASTPLATE OF RIGHTEOUSNESS"

It's not a good idea to stop a sword-thrust with your bare chest. The breastplate protects your heart, and it's very hard to function without a heart.

The breastplate of righteousness is our being made right before God by our faith in Jesus Christ. When we live a godly life by the power of the Holy Spirit, we block Satan's accusations against us. He loves to bring up our past and remind us of our sins, but in Christ we are forgiven and free. Next time Satan tries to bring up your past, just remind him of his future.

The way we live either fortifies us against Satan's attacks or makes it easier for him to defeat us.

"THE READINESS THAT COMES FROM THE GOSPEL OF PEACE"

Imagine trying to run, jump, hop, and fight across rocks, thorns, and thistles without sandals. Soon you'd prefer sitting to fighting. We need to be at peace with God and others. When we're at peace, we're ready for any temptation or attack. We can move and react swiftly, and we are prepared to share Jesus Christ with those whom Satan holds captive.

"THE SHIELD OF FAITH"

Have you ever tried to stop an axe blow with your bare arm? If you forget to carry your shield into battle, everyone will start saying, "Hey, there goes old One Arm."

Shields used to be wooden and covered with leather. They were about four feet by two feet, and the edges were made in such a way that an entire line of soldiers could interlock their shields and march into the enemy as a solid line. So the shield of faith reminds us that we are not alone. Hundreds of thousands of Christians all over the world stand with us. Imagine the impact we could have if one day we interlocked our shields and marched against Satan together!

Faith is believing that God is able to do what He says. Faith is applying the promises of God to our lives. It protects us from Satan's fiery arrows of doubt, lies, blasphemous thoughts, evil desires, and the like. Right now Satan is taking aim, so grab your shield!

"THE HELMET OF SALVATION"

The helmet protects the head. All of your actions, convictions, and beliefs begin in your mind. If Satan can pervert your mind, he can pervert your actions.

The helmet of salvation is a mind controlled by God. We act as He would have us act and speak as He would have us speak. This will only happen if our mind is surrendered to the Holy Spirit.

The helmet is also the assurance that we are saved. We don't have to worry about where we are going to spend eternity. We are free to love and serve Him. When God is in control of our mind, it is very difficult for Satan to lead us astray.

"THE SWORD OF THE SPIRIT"

A sword of steel pierces the body, but the spiritual sword pierces the heart. A physical sword kills, but the spiritual sword inflicts wounds of healing and gives life.

It's important to use the Word of God when we talk with others. It makes a much greater impact than merely our thoughts and opinions.

We should also use the sword when we deal with Satan. This is one of our primary offensive weapons. The Word of God inflicts a lot of damage on Satan and his demons.

The forces of evil hate the Word of God. When dealing with individuals who are demonically controlled, *always* read the Word of God. Usually the demons cause the person to cover his or her ears because it hurts them to hear it. Demons HATE the Word of God. If we have a weapon that can hurt Satan, doesn't it make sense to take advantage of it?

We need to study, understand, memorize, and apply the Word to our lives. If you don't memorize the Scriptures and you get attacked when you don't have access to a Bible, you will be defenseless.

"Pray in the Spirit on All Occasions"

Prayer is our other offensive weapon. It can strike damaging blows against the forces of evil and destroy their strongholds.

Satan and his demons tremble when we get down on our knees and earnestly seek God in prayer. Unfortunately, we don't pray enough. *I* don't pray enough. However, that doesn't mean we can't change.

Try this: think of the names of one non-Christian friend and one carnal Christian friend. They should be individuals who could do tremendous damage to Satan's domain if they turned their lives over to Jesus Christ.

Non-Christian _____

Carnal Christian _____

Whenever you are under attack, pray that these two individuals will come to Christ. When you do that, you are advancing into Satan's very territory and attacking him. We need to take the offensive.

We need to pray for each other and support one another. It is said of Christians that we are the only army in the world that shoots its wounded. We have to stop attacking each other and start praying for each other.

"Be Alert"

Be alert, and don't put yourself in a position where you become vulnerable to Satan.

When we put on the full armor of God, we are really taking upon ourselves the Lord Jesus Christ.

"Clothe yourselves with the Lord Jesus Christ, and do not think about how to gratify the desires of the sinful nature" (Romans 13:14).

Whenever you make a commitment to God, the first thirty days will be the toughest. When you come back from a retreat or summer camp, the first thirty days are crucial. Why? Because that's when Satan hits you the hardest. He doesn't want you to get established in obeying God, so he does everything he can to discourage you right away. Satan's greatest nightmare is that teenagers come alive, follow Christ, live holy lives, and fight on God's side in spiritual warfare.

I'm going to leave you with a quote from John Wesley, but I'm going to change the word *men* to *teenagers* (sorry, John). "Give me one hundred teenagers who love only God with all their hearts and hate only sin with all their hearts and we will shake the gates of hell and bring the Kingdom of God to this generation."

Will you be one of those hundred?

QUOTES

If the devil could be persuaded to write a Bible, he would title it "You Only Live Once!"

(Sidney Harris)

The devil can cite Scripture for his purpose.

(William Shakespeare)

The devil's greatest asset is the doubt people have about his existence.

(John Nicola)

I believe Satan to exist for two reasons: first the Bible says so; and second, I've done business with him.

(D. L. Moody)

13

Suffering—A Promise
We Don't Like to Claim

In junior high there was a girl who liked me. But in junior high no one says, "I like you. Do you like me?" That would be too scary. Instead, you try to get that person's attention, or you tell someone to tell someone, who tells someone to tell someone, who tells that person that you like him/her.

One day, I was standing at my opened locker talking with a friend. The girl who liked me walked by, and she decided that she wanted to get my attention. She thought it would be funny if she slammed my locker shut. I would yell, and she would giggle with her friends, and—best of all—she would get noticed.

Then I would like her, and since she already liked me, everything would be great. We would meet for dates at the mall. I would give her a ring or an ID bracelet or nose hair. We would go steady and fall deeply in love. Finally, we would break up—all in about one week. It made sense.

So there I was, innocently talking to my friend. She walked by, stuck out her hand, and faster than you can say, "Greg, you are going to suffer," slammed my locker as hard as she could. At that point, everything would have gone as planned, except for one slight problem. I had my hand in my locker.

She slammed that door right across my knuckles. It hurt so bad I wanted to die, but after a little while, I just wanted her to die. Needless to say, I didn't like her, we didn't meet at the mall, and I didn't give her anything, although I would have been happy to give her a fat lip.

On the suffering scale that incident was pretty minor. But it shows that if we aren't prepared for suffering, we will find ourselves slipping in our relationship with Jesus when it happens.

Let's go back to the beginning of suffering.

In the beginning, God's creation was good and perfect (see Genesis 1:31). There was no sickness, suffering, or death. God only asked one thing of Adam and Eve—not to eat from the tree of the knowledge of good and evil. That wasn't too much to ask! And He told them what would happen if they did: "When you eat of it you will surely die" (Genesis 2:17). If they disobeyed, death and suffering would enter the world. Did Adam and Eve listen? Noooo!

"When the woman saw that the fruit of the tree was good for food and pleasing to the eye, and also desirable for gaining wisdom, she took some and ate it. She also gave some to her husband, who was with her, and he ate it" (Genesis 3:6). At that moment suffering and death entered the world. The fruit was not evil, but the act itself was. They disobeyed God.

"Couldn't God have made it so we wouldn't sin at all?" Yes, but then we wouldn't be human; we'd be robots programmed to act and react in certain ways. God gives us the awesome privilege and responsibility to make choices. We can choose to obey or disobey, but like Adam and Eve in the Garden, there are consequences to our choices.

"OK, why doesn't God just destroy all evil?" Because He would have to do a complete job of it. Let's say God decided to destroy all evil at noon tomorrow. At 12:01 how many of us would be left?

So what's God doing about suffering? The good news is that He already did something. He sent His Son Jesus Christ into the world to suffer and die for us. Christ suffered so that we could have inner peace and joy in the midst of suffering and chaos.

What causes suffering?

☐ Satan

Satan finds great pleasure in causing suffering and pain. Although his power is limited, Satan does cause some of the suffering in the world.

☐ People

Someone does a poor job constructing a building, and it falls down. Bad wiring causes a plane to crash. A drunk driver gets into a serious accident. A woman uses drugs, and her baby is born deformed. Are those things God's fault? No. They are the fault of people. We cause each other terrible suffering.

☐ God's discipline

"Do not be deceived: God cannot be mocked. A man reaps what he sows. The one who sows to please his sinful nature, from that nature will reap destruction; the one who sows to please the Spirit, from the Spirit will reap eternal life" (Galatians 6:7-8). That is a warning we shouldn't take lightly. Sometimes God allows us to suffer as He disciplines us so that we might repent. Discipline is part of love, and God disciplines those He loves.

Suffering is never easy, but let me give you five basic principles from Scripture to help you cope with it.

DON'T BE SURPRISED BY SUFFERING

We have the misconception that when we come to Jesus and commit ourselves to Him, we won't have any more problems. We think everything will be wonderful all the time. If that has been your attitude, let me be the first to welcome you back to reality.

"Dear friends, do not be surprised at the painful trial you are suffering, as though something strange were happening to you. But rejoice that you participate in the sufferings of Christ, so that you may be overjoyed when His glory is revealed" (1 Peter 4:12-13; also see John 16:33).

There are different degrees of suffering. We think suffering is being tortured by a huge guy ripping off our fingernails. That would certainly be suffering, but maybe we can better relate to some other forms.

☐ People laughing at you because you are a Christian
☐ Losing a good friend
☐ Emotional, sexual, and physical abuse
☐ Sickness
☐ Having your feelings hurt
☐ Failure
☐ A loved one's dying

Let's say you invite me to your house for a steak dinner. We've been talking and having a wonderful time. But in the middle of the conversation there is one of those awkward silences when nobody knows what to say, so you all stuff food in your mouths to avoid having to say anything.

Suddenly, I let out a blood-curdling scream. Your father spits out his food, you suck an entire beet down your throat, and your mother passes out face-

down in the mashed potatoes. Everyone eventually recovers, and the first thing you decide is that you'll never have me over for dinner again.

What if I decided to scream again, but I warned you ahead of time? I'd say, "I'm going to scream at the count of three. Get ready, prepare yourself, here we go. One, two, three . . . AUGGHHH!"

It would still be unpleasant, but it wouldn't surprise you because you'd be expecting it. When we don't prepare ourselves to suffer, we are caught off-guard. That doesn't have to be the case. You can't always control your circumstances, but you can control your attitude. You can choose to remain joyful regardless of what is happening around you. Don't be surprised by suffering (2 Timothy 3:12)!

SUFFERING WILL DEVELOP YOU

"We also rejoice in our sufferings, because we know that suffering produces perseverance; persever-

ance, character; and character, hope" (Romans 5:3-
4).
   Our problem is that we assume suffering is bad.
But through suffering and pain we grow. God uses
suffering for our good. If He shielded us from pain, He
would be robbing us of a chance to mature.
   Scripture talks about some positive characteristics
that will be developed in our lives through suffering.

☐ Perseverance
   We can't have a give-up attitude. We must be
steadfast and strong. We cannot tire of doing what's
right even when it's hard. We want to feel good,
and we want it right now! So we take the path of
least resistance.
   But Christians want to develop a good relationship with God and influence others positively.
That doesn't happen by taking the path of least resistance! Instead, you work at your life. It's hard,
but you don't give up. When suffering comes, you
don't run away; you stick around and learn from
it.

☐ Character
   We desperately need men and women of character today. We have lots of intellectual giants who
are moral midgets. D. L. Moody defined character
as "what a man does in the dark."
   Suffering reveals our character. There is nothing like a problem to show us what our faith in
God really is. It's easy to follow God and love Him
when things are going well, but what do you do
when life doesn't seem fair?
   My favorite movie of all time is *Chariots of Fire*.
One of the reasons I love it is a man named Eric
Liddell. He was a Scottish runner on the Olympic

team who loved God with all his heart. His race was the 100-yard dash, but he discovered that the preliminaries for that race were to be run on a Sunday. He didn't believe in running on Sunday because it was a day of worship and rest. Instead of compromising his principles—even though it was the Olympics—he decided not to run.

Obviously he had to put up with a lot of persecution and abuse for that decision. But he stood his ground and refused to compromise. And God opened another window of opportunity. A friend of his was entered in the 440, and he volunteered to let Eric run in his place because he had already won a medal. The only problem was that the greatest runner in the world, an American, was also in that race.

So there's Eric in the Olympics, about to run the 440. He had been training for the 100-yard dash, which is a very different race. To switch events like that would be totally unheard of today.

The American runner is getting ready for the finals when his coach comes up to encourage him. The American asks, "What about Liddell?"

His coach says, "Don't worry about Liddell. He's a sprinter, and he'll die in the last seventy-five yards."

So the American runner is feeling good. Coach leaves, and another U.S. runner comes up to him. "Watch out for Liddell," he says.

"What? Coach said not to worry because he's a sprinter and will die in the end."

The other runner says, "Eric Liddell has something that men like Coach don't know anything about."

Eric not only beat the American runner, but he beat all the other runners as well and won the Olympic gold!

Eric Liddell was a man of character. What did he have that "men like Coach don't know anything about"? A deep love and commitment to Jesus Christ.

When we become men and women of character, we rise above difficult situations to honor and glorify Jesus Christ.

☐ Hope

Perseverance and character lead to hope. Hope is not a bunch of warm fuzzies. It's not empty optimism about tomorrow. Hope is assurance in an all-powerful and all-knowing God, who holds our lives in His hand.

When people become missionaries they give up comfort, stability, wealth, and in some cases their lives to serve Christ. How can they do that? Because they have hope in something bigger than nice houses, hot cars, expensive clothes, and the right crowd. Their hope is in the King of kings.

Back in the old days, long before I was born, goldsmiths used to refine gold. They put gold in large vats and started a fire under each vat. Temperature was very important; if it got too hot, it would destroy the gold, but if it was too cold, the gold would harden. It had to be just the right temperature so all the impurities would rise to the surface. The goldsmith would stand over the vat and scoop away those impurities. He knew the gold was ready when he could look into the vat and see a clear reflection of himself in the gold.

That's what Jesus does in our lives. He allows problems and suffering to purify us. He doesn't want it to be so hard that it destroys us, but He doesn't want it to be so easy that we become apathetic. It has to be just the right temperature so all the impurities such as jealousy, hate, lust, rebellion, and bitterness rise to the surface.

SUFFERING IS ONLY TEMPORARY

"The God of all grace, who called you to his eternal glory in Christ, after you have suffered a little while, will himself restore you and make you strong, firm and steadfast" (1 Peter 5:10).

There is a light at the end of the tunnel. Your suffering will end, even if you have suffered every day for the past seventy-five years. One day Christ will take you home to glory, and you will be freed of sickness, suffering, pain, and tears. The suffering that you endure here on earth will be nothing compared to the wonder and riches of heaven.

JESUS CHRIST SUFFERED

When it comes to suffering God is not distant or aloof. No suffering has come to us that hasn't just passed through the heart and hand of God (Isaiah 53:3; Hebrews 2:18). Most of us will never suffer to the extent that Christ did, but when we do suffer, we can have the confidence that Christ understands and has the power to help us.

Let's take a closer look at Christ's suffering.

☐ "Jesus was troubled in spirit and testified, 'I tell you the truth, one of you is going to betray me'" (John 13:21). Imagine knowing that one of your closest friends for the past three years is going to turn you over to be tortured and killed. Christ knew, and it hurt Him.

☐ "Then some began to spit at him; they blindfolded him, struck him with their fists, and said, 'Prophesy!' And the guards took him and beat him (Mark 14:65; see Matthew 26:68; Luke 22:65). Christ was taken before Caiaphas and the Sanhedrin. The trial was a legal joke. Afterward, He was taken outside, and the Roman soldiers and Temple guards were free to abuse Him.

They started by spitting on Him, which is incredibly gross and humiliating. Then they decided to play a cruel game. They blindfolded Him and hit Him one at a time. They weren't just slapping Him, they were hitting Him with their fists. Laughing, they'd ask Jesus to tell them who landed the blow.

Christ couldn't protect Himself. He couldn't even see what direction they were coming from or how hard they were swinging or where they would hit Him next. The force of the blows probably knocked Him down.

When they couldn't get a rise out of Jesus they got more angry. Finally the guards decided to get serious and beat Him severely. Soon Christ's face was covered with spit, blood, dirt, and sweat. That would be enough for most of us to quit and give up. But for Christ it was only the beginning.

☐ "Then Pilate took Jesus and had him flogged" (John 19:1). The guards made Jesus face a large post, removed His clothes, and tied His hands above His head to the post. A Roman soldier began to hit Him with a whip consisting of several heavy leather straps. At the bottom of each leather strap were pieces of lead, bone, and chain. He hit Jesus over and over and over again on the shoulders, back, and legs. With each blow, pieces of flesh were torn away. When He was hit across the shoulders, part of the whip wrapped around His neck, gashing His face. Finally, the skin on His back, shoulders, and legs was hanging in shreds. His back was an unrecognizable mass of bleeding flesh and muscle. Many men died from those beatings, although that was not the Romans' purpose. They wanted to bring their victims to the point of death and then revive them. If we had witnessed that, many of us would have fainted or vomited.

☐ "The soldiers twisted together a crown of thorns and put it on his head. They clothed him in a purple robe and went up to Him again and again, saying, 'Hail, king of the Jews!' And they struck Him in the face" (John 19:2-3). Long, large thorns dug into His scalp. They placed a robe on His shoulders, but even that must have hurt as it touched raw, bleeding flesh. They mocked, ridiculed, and insulted Him. Again, they struck Him in the face.

Can you see Satan standing there with his demons, laughing with glee at each insult and dancing with delight at each blow laid upon the Son of God?

Meanwhile in the distance stood twelve legions of angels (about seventy-two thousand; Matthew 26:53). They probably stood in silence. Some wept, and others gritted their teeth. Each stood ready and waiting for Jesus to call.

The demons dared not get too close, but they probably called out, laughed, and insulted Him from a distance.

Leading the forces of light was Michael, the archangel. "Just say the word, Jesus, and faster than lightning we will rescue and avenge You."

But He never did, and the demons danced as the angels waited.

☐ "They brought Jesus to the place called Golgotha (which means The Place of the Skull). Then they offered him wine mixed with myrrh, but he did not take it. And they crucified him" (Mark 15:22-24). Sounds pretty simple, doesn't it? "And they crucified him." Do you know what happens when a man is crucified?

Jesus was stripped of His clothes, except for a loincloth. He was thrown against the cross, and the solders nailed His hands. They felt for the depression in the wrist and pounded a heavy, square, iron nail through each wrist into the wood. It definitely wasn't a nice pointed nail. The legionnaire hit the nail once, and it broke into the wrist. He hit it a second time, and it pushed through to the other side of the wrist. On the third hit, it broke through the wrist into the wood, and the fourth and fifth hits secured the nail into the wood.

The feet were more difficult. They had to make sure His knees were bent and His feet were flat against the wood. They put one foot on top of the other and pounded a long spike through both feet into the wood.

The cross was then lifted into place. Jesus Christ was now crucified.

As He slowly sank down, all His weight hung from His wrists. Horrible, fiery pain shot up His arms to explode into His brain. To relieve that pain, He had to push up on the spike through His feet—more terrible pain as the nail tore through nerves in His feet. Up and down He would move, His mutilated back rubbing off chunks of flesh on the rough timber. Waves of cramps swept over His body, paralyzing His muscles as they knotted in throbbing pain.

When the cramps came, He couldn't push up anymore, so He had to hang by His arms. In that position, he could inhale, but not exhale. Between cramps, He had to fight to push up on His feet, so He could exhale and bring in the oxygen that He so desperately needed.

☐ "My God, my God, why have you forsaken me?" (Matthew 27:46). Until the crucifixion, the Father, Son, and Holy Spirit had always had close fellowship and communion with one another. But now God turned His back on Jesus because He had become total sin. The vast wall that had separated man from God now separated Jesus from His Father. This was the greatest suffering of all.

The legions of angels probably withdrew as well. Jesus was utterly and completely alone. Surrounding Him was darkness, hate, wickedness, and evil. Hordes of demons and even Satan himself watched God's only Son die.

Next time you start thinking it's too hard to serve Jesus, remember what He did for you on the cross! Few of us will have to suffer as He did. But would we? Before you say yes, tell me how you have stood up to laughter, mocking, loneliness, rejection, and emotional suffering for the cause of Christ. If we say we are willing to die for Jesus, we must first be willing to live for Him.

THE VICTORY IS OURS

"Those who suffer according to God's will should commit themselves to their faithful Creator and continue to do good" (1 Peter 4:19).

What do you do in the midst of suffering? Don't give in or run away. You are tempted to become angry, bitter, and discouraged, but that doesn't do any good either. Instead, take two positive steps.

☐ Commit yourself to God.

If anybody understands your suffering, God does. He wants you to grow through difficult times. Suffering can help you become more godly and draw closer to Him.

Instead of turning away from God in anger and resentment, turn toward Him. Again, study the Bible, pray, get back to church, and allow Christian friends to encourage you. Ask the Holy Spirit to fill and control you. God is faithful, and He WILL heal you. If not in this life, then for sure in the next.

☐ Do good!

When we are hurting, we have a tendency to want attention. We want others to serve us. Look

around; there are a lot of people hurting. You need to reach out to those people and serve them.

We have the VICTORY in Christ, right now. The war has already been won; we are just fighting a few battles. So do good to those around you, and you'll begin to feel better about your situation.

You'll also find that as you do good to others, others will begin to do good to you. You don't have to scheme, plan, and manipulate to get attention. Just trust the Lord!

QUOTES

A Christian is someone who shares the sufferings of God in the world.

(Dietrich Bonhoeffer)

We are not in this world simply to enjoy God's gifts. We are here to use them in building of His kingdom, which calls for some kind of suffering.

(Arnold G. Kuntz)

Adversity does not make us frail, it only shows us how frail we are.

(Abraham Lincoln)

The real problem is not why some pious, humble, believing people suffer, but why some do not.

(C. S. Lewis)

14

Love—Be a Lover

I was dating a wonderful woman in California who will remain anonymous because I wouldn't want her to be humiliated when her friends discover that she dated me. I'll call her Debbie.

I went off to college with her picture in my wallet and her love in my heart. But at college I met another woman, whom I'll call Shirley. I was kind of lonely, so I thought, *One is from California, and the other is from Minnesota. They will never meet, so I won't say a word. I can seriously date both of them.*

All the women reading this now think I'm a total jerk, but that's what love does. It causes you to do stupid things.

Everything was going great. Valentine's Day was coming up, so I went to the store to buy two cards.

I hate shopping for cards. It is so hard to find one that doesn't sound idiotic! There I was, reading Valentine cards that said

> We're good friends and it's Valentine's Day.
> 10 pounds of chocolate for you, I would pay
> Or I thought about a big fudge cat,
> But then I realized you're already too fat.
> HAPPY VALENTINE'S DAY

or

My love for you is a burning fire
To kiss your lips was my big desire
But too early, my eyes, I did close
I missed your lips and sucked your nose.
HAPPY VALENTINE'S DAY

After twenty minutes of reading that stuff, I *finally* found a card that was pretty good. I asked myself, *Greg, do you want to stand here for another twenty minutes looking for another card? NO!*

Instead, I had a brilliant idea. I could buy the same card for both women. They were hundreds of miles away from each other. The same card expressed my feelings for both of them, and it would save me twenty minutes. So I bought two.

About one week before Valentine's Day, I sat down and wrote in the cards. I poured out my feelings to each girl. I told each one how much she meant to me, how much I cared about her, how fortunate I was to have a girlfriend like her.

When I finished, I left the room for a minute. But I came right back and put each card in its envelope. I left Shirley's Valentine on the corner of my desk, and I sealed Deb's and mailed it.

Valentine's Day finally came. I was going to spend some time with Shirley, so picked up her card. I wanted to personally hand it to her.

But it had been a few days, and I decided to read the card again to make sure I said exactly what I'd wanted to say. I opened the letter and began to read. "Dear Deb . . ."

My heart stopped. My life passed before my eyes, my mouth dropped open, sweat ran down my arm, and I froze. I had sent Shirley's card to Deb! All I could think was *Come, Lord Jesus.*

I pled insanity. Love made me do it.

Is that true? Infatuation may cause us to do incredibly stupid things, but we usually blame it on love.

What does it really mean to love one another?

Let's say you and I are talking together. I turn to you and say, "Look, I want you to know that I really appreciate you and love you." I smile, you smile—and then I slug you in the stomach as hard as I can. You double over and fall on the floor.

I help you back up on the couch and say, "Wow, I'm really sorry, but I want you to know that I do love you." You're gasping for breath when I slap you across the face. You fall over backward, and your face is stinging. As you lie on the floor, you think, *He doesn't really love me.*

Why would you say that? For several reasons.

LOVE IS ACTION

If our actions don't back up our words, our words are useless. "Dear children, let us not love with words or tongue but with actions and in truth" (1 John 3:18). We need to show people that we love them, as God showed us. What does John 3:16 say? "For God so loved the world that he shouted at it"? No, it says, "For God so loved the world that he gave his one and only Son." God saw our need, and He sent His Son as a result of His love. Our love must always lead us to action.

People say to me, "My favorite chapter in the Bible is first Corinthians thirteen."

"Why?" I ask.

"Well, because it's about love, and I just think love is wonderful!"

"Are you living out first Corinthians thirteen?"

"Huh?"

First Corinthians 13 *is* a wonderful chapter. But if it's only nice-sounding words on a page, it won't make much of a difference in your life. Let's take a closer look at it.

☐ Love is patient (Proverbs 16:32).
  Love waits calmly and endures for long periods of time. It doesn't easily lose its temper, become irritable, or angry. When you love, you are not in a hurry because you know that God has everything under control.

☐ Love is kind (Proverbs 14:21).
  Love looks for ways to constructively help others. It fully accepts others in spite of their shortcomings. It creatively finds ways to serve. It is sensitive to needs.

☐ Love doesn't envy (Proverbs 14:30).
  Love is not jealous; it doesn't plot against someone else. It's not possessive, nor does it try to control other people's lives.

☐ Love doesn't boast (Proverbs 27:11).
  Love doesn't brag. It isn't quick to bring up past accomplishments or talk about planned future accomplishments. It doesn't seek to build itself up. Love boasts only of the Lord.

☐ Love isn't proud (Proverbs 16:5).
  Love isn't arrogant. It isn't self-centered and knows that life doesn't revolve around it. Love doesn't demand its own way, and it is willing to lay down its rights for someone else.

☐ Love isn't rude (Proverbs 15:30).
  Love is not indecent or shameful. It always respect others and shows good manners. It thinks before it speaks and does not purposely hurt others.

☐ Love isn't self-seeking (Proverbs 18:1).
   Love does not insist on its own way. It doesn't seek to make self number one. Love is always open and available to be used by God.

☐ Love isn't easily angered (Proverbs 29:11).
   Love is not touchy. It doesn't take things too personally or get into stupid arguments. Love gets angry at things that are worth getting angry about —sin, evil, and Satan.

☐ Love doesn't keep a record of wrongs (Proverbs 10:12).
   When you love, you don't make a list of all the wrongs done to you. You are quick to forgive and don't hold the past over someone else's head.

☐ Love does not delight in evil (Proverbs 8:13).
   Love does not use other people's evil to justify poor behavior. Love never excuses evil, no matter what the result. It counters by doing good. Love rejoices when right overcomes wrong.

☐ Love always protects (Proverbs 14:16).
   Love looks out for the underdog. It cares about the rights and feelings of others. It takes an interest in the problems and hurts of others. Love can be counted on in a crisis.

☐ Love trusts (Proverbs 3:5-6).
   Love believes in God completely. It always believes the best about others. It listens, understands, and believes.

☐ Love hopes (Proverbs 23:18).
   Love knows that eternity awaits, so it doesn't fade or become dismayed, no matter what the external conditions.

☐ Love perseveres (Proverbs 27:24).
Riches and fame will all fade away, but love endures to the end of time. It never gives up on God
or anyone else. It's tough, making decisions that
may wound someone temporarily but in the long
run will prove to be healing. It does not weaken
even when immediate results are not seen. It out-
lasts everything else and continues even when there
is no love in return.

Love Is Unconditional

Love must be tough. We are called to love the unlovely. "But I tell you who hear me: Love your enemies, do good to those who hate you, bless those who
curse you, pray for those who mistreat you" (Luke
6:27). We are to love those who are poor, smelly, geeky,
angry, selfish, obnoxious, immature, gross, and all-
around pains.

After I finished college, I worked at a home for
delinquent and emotionally disturbed teenagers. It
was a great place to practice unconditional love.
Many of the teens were right off the streets, and they
were hard.

When a kid arrived at the home, I would shake
his hand, say, "Welcome to the unit," and put my
arm around him. He usually pulled away.

I would wait a few days, then put my arm around
him and say, "How are you doing?" He'd pull away a
little more fiercely and say, "Take your hands off me!"

If I reacted the way the world had reacted to him,
I would have said, "Fine, you don't touch me, and I
won't touch you. Stay away from me, and I'll stay
away from you." But God calls us to love with tough
love. So I would wait a little longer and then go back
to him, put my arm around him, and say, "What's

happening?" He would pull away and say, "Hey, do you have a problem? Don't touch me!"

That would continue for a week or a month or sometimes longer. Then one day I'd approach that individual, put my arm around him, and say, "How are you doing?" And he would put his arm around me and say, "Fine, how are you?"

Do we love unconditionally? We can't love with ulterior motives. Once again, our example is Jesus. "A man with leprosy came and knelt before him and said, 'Lord, if you are willing, you can make me clean.' Jesus reached out his hand and touched the man. 'I am willing,' he said. 'Be clean!' Immediately he was cured of his leprosy" (Matthew 8:1-3).

Imagine that leper kneeling before Jesus. What could he give Jesus? Was the leper physically attractive? Be serious; he'd make the elephant man look good.

How about money? He was poorer than poor.

Popularity? He was alone. No one hung around with him, except other lepers. Nobody said, "Hey, let's go hang out with Larry the leper."

But what was Christ's reply? "I am willing." In other words He said, "I want to love you. Not just if you can give Me something or because we share some common interests, but because I love you unconditionally!"

Some kids at your school would like to cry out and say, "If you're willing you can change my life!" We have to break out of our wolf packs and reach out to others. If you want to, you can allow Christ to work through you to love the unlovely.

Love Isn't Merely a Feeling

It's nice to feel warm and fuzzy inside, but feelings are not the foundation of love.

You are at a party, and you look across this crowded room and see him/her. Your eyes meet, and for a moment the world stands still. You float across the room into each other's arms. You're in love! You can't eat, sleep, or study (yea!) because you are overwhelmed with emotion.

I have terrible news. As quickly as you fall in love, you can fall out of love. One day you will float across the room, take that special person in your arms, and say, "Oh, ohhh . . . ish! That's a huge pimple! Wow, it's right between your eyes. It looks like a second nose. Hey, have you gained weight?" All of a sudden the fuzzy feelings end, and the next time you feel them, they're for someone else.

But love isn't just a bunch of gushy gooey feelings—it's a commitment. Love is something you do whether you feel like it or not.

If we could go back to the cross where Jesus hung, we could ask Him, "Jesus, does it feel good to hang on this cross?" He would say, "No, but because I love you, I'll stay."

It's easy to give away canned goods or throw a couple of bucks into an offering plate. I'm not minimizing the importance of helping, but we like to do it the easy way so it doesn't cost us much. We forget that Jesus Christ calls us to love individuals: mother, father, brother, sister, neighbor, teacher.

You say, "Look, I love Jesus, but my parents are a pain, and I'm not going to love them."

Then you don't really love the Lord! "If anyone says, 'I love God,' yet hates his brother, he is a liar. For anyone who does not love his brother, whom he has seen, cannot love God, whom he has not seen" (1 John 4:20).

How Do I Love?

The world says, "If you're a real man/woman, you won't show any emotion or love because that is weakness. Put up masks and walls; steel yourself."

Baloney! That is not the description of a real anything.

My parents taught me a lot about true love and vulnerability. I grew up in California, but I went to college in Minnesota. When I'd come home from college on breaks, my parents would be at the airport to greet me. When I got off the plane, my father did *not* walk over to me solemnly, shake my hand, and say, "Hello, son. Welcome home. You remember your mother, don't you? Come over and say hi."

When my father saw me getting off the plane, he would get a big smile on his face. In front of a hundred people, he'd give me a big hug and say, "Greg, I

love you." And I would say, "I love you, too." I had a great father.

Is that weakness? Actually it is tremendous strength. How do you aggressively reach out and show love? Here are five practical ways.

☐ With words

Today we think it's cool to rip on one another. We cut each other down, and then what do we say? "I was just kidding. Come on, can't you take a joke?" Let's get rid of the sarcasm and build each other up.

When is the last time you said I love you to your parents? Sure, they make mistakes. But no matter how your parents act, God commands you to love them.

Try this: when you're around other people, compliment them about at least one thing. Make it natural. Whatever you do, don't be phony. Don't say, "I just love your double chin and the way it hangs over your turtleneck." That is not a good compliment.

You may not realize how much a kind word can mean to a person. Back in high school, I played football. We had practices twice a day in the summer, and that meant the temperature was in the nineties. One afternoon I was dragging in from practice, with sweat pouring out of my pores, and I was thinking, *What am I doing here? Is this worth it?*

My coach walked by and said three words that changed my day. He slapped me on the rear and said, "Good job, Speck!" That was all. But he changed my day. Somebody had noticed all my hard work and was willing to take the time to compliment me.

Give one or two people who aren't close friends a call each week just to see how they are doing and encourage them. One of the best ways to love people with words is to pray with and for them. Words are a great way to communicate love!

☐ Giving gifts

"A woman came with an alabaster jar of very expensive perfume, made of pure nard. She broke the jar and poured the perfume on his head" (Mark 14:3). A woman expressed her love for Jesus by giving Him expensive perfume.

When you give someone a gift, you are communicating that you care about him or her. You are also saying, "When we are apart I think of you."

You can buy gifts, but in most cases if they are hand-made they're even nicer. They don't have to be elaborate or expensive.

It was the end of my senior year at Bethel, and I was having a bad day. Finals were coming up, and I had papers due, plus the minor consideration of figuring out what I was going to do with the rest of my life.

I went to my post office box even though it was usually empty. I whipped it open and—a miracle! There was something inside.

I pulled out a three-by-five-inch card that said, "Hi, Greg. Have a great day! Love, Me." I reached back in the box and pulled out an orange. Someone had colored a big, beautiful smiley face on it. I just stood there and stared at the card and the orange. I turned to the people next to me and said, "Hey, look! I got an orange, and it came with a card, and it's for me!"

I took the card and the orange back to my room. I put them both on my desk and kept them there

212 Living for Jesus When the Party's Over

until the orange rotted beyond recognition. My day had been changed because someone cared enough about me to color an orange and write out a card.

Sometimes the best time to give gifts is when it isn't a holiday. If you give a gift when it's not Christmas, a birthday, anniversary, Easter, or Groundhog Day, it's even more special because no one is expecting anything.

When was the last time you took your mother flowers? "Aw, Greg, I can't afford flowers!" Give me a break. I'm not talking about a dozen long-stemmed roses. Buy your mother one daisy or carnation. It's not what you spend that's important; it's that you are thinking about her.

Another easy, inexpensive gift is a note. My wife does that for me. She writes me notes and hides them in my briefcase. You could do that for your friends and parents. Place a note in a book, on the bathroom mirror, in the refrigerator, in the car, in a locker. Use your imagination, and love someone by giving a gift.

☐ Doing things for others

"If someone forces you to go one mile, go with him two miles" (Matthew 5:41). That verse is talking about doing more than what is expected of you; it's talking about being a servant.

To serve someone is to give that person the opportunity to receive not only your love but also the love of God. Take the initiative to serve. You should be 100 percent responsible, 100 percent of the time. Don't wait for someone else to set up the chairs or clean up or whatever—*you* do it.

☐ Spending time together
A great way to communicate love is by being willing to listen. Most of us love to talk, and few of us are willing to take the time to listen. When you listen, you make someone else feel significant.

Here is a scary experiment. Once a week at school decide that you are not going to eat with your friends. Pray about it, and ask God to send someone to eat with you who could use some encouragement or to point out someone who is lonely whom you could help.

☐ By touch
"Then he touched their eyes and said, 'According to your faith will it be done to you'" (Matthew 9:29). Notice how often Jesus touched people. Touch is a wonderful way to communicate love. To give someone a hug or pat on the back is to say, "You are special."

Now, a word of warning. In all of those ways of showing love, we have to be careful about male-female relationships. Our love needs to be pure. If we are doing any of those things because we're trying to hit on someone, that is wrong.

Start loving the people around you, beginning with your family. The only thing that will limit you is your creativity. I want you to think of the names of three people who need love. Spend time in prayer, and God will lay some names on your heart. Write them down, and then pick a way to show love to each of them. Write down specifically what you are going to do. Then do it this week. Keep it up, week after week, month after month. It's contagious!

	Name	Act of Love
1.	_____	_____
2.	_____	_____
3.	_____	_____

Who was the greatest lover that ever lived? It wasn't Casanova, Don Juan, or even Greg Speck (why is my wife laughing?). The greatest lover that ever lived was Jesus Christ. Be a lover. Be like Him!

QUOTES

Yes, love is the magic key of life—not to get what we want, but to become what we ought to be.

(Eileen Guder)

There are more people who wish to be loved than there are willing to love.

(S. R. N. Chamfort)

People don't go where the action is, they go where love is.

(Jess Moody)

The final test of love is obedience.

(A. W. Tozer)

We are shaped and fashioned by what we love.

(Johann Wolfgang von Goethe)

15

Final Thoughts

Emotions never last, but your walk with Christ will, if you develop it and depend upon the Holy Spirit. Hang in there, and don't give up. Together we will follow the Lord and serve Him. By the power of the Holy Spirit we can shake the gates of hell and bring the kingdom of God to this generation. Our God is an awesome God!

"For the Lord your God is God of gods and Lord of lords, the great God, mighty and awesome, who shows no partiality and accepts no bribes" (Deuteronomy 10:17).

Try applying the ideas in this book to your life, then let me know what happens. I read every letter and respond to each one personally. Let me know if I can help or encourage you. My address is on the next page.

218 Living for Jesus When the Party's Over

Other Materials available from Greg Speck:

Cassette tapes for $6 each:

Dating, Sex and You
Parents, Friend or Foe?
Satan, Know Your Enemy
Not Guilty
School, Don't Waste It
Self-Image, You Are Beautiful
Goliath and the Freshman
Dealing with Depression

Other resources

Sex, It's Worth Waiting For (book)
It's Worth Waiting For (video series)

If you are interested in joining Greg and Royal Servants for a summer missions trip, write to Greg and request a brochure.

Order video series and cassettes from:

Greg Speck
6859 Millbrook Dr.
Rockford, IL 61108
815-399-0680

Please make checks payable to Greg Speck.